The Financial Integration and Resilience Model

American Alliance of Museums

The American Alliance of Museums has been bringing museums together since 1906, helping to develop standards and best practices, gathering and sharing knowledge, and providing advocacy on issues of concern to the entire museum community. Representing more than 35,000 individual museum professionals and volunteers, institutions, and corporate partners serving the museum field, the Alliance stands for the broad scope of the museum community.

The American Alliance of Museums' mission is to champion museums and nurture excellence in partnership with its members and allies.

Books published by AAM further the Alliance's mission to make standards and best practices for the broad museum community widely available.

American Alliance of Museums

The Financial Integration and Resilience Model

Building the Museum Financial Ecosystem

Ashley Amos and Jon Carver

BLOOMSBURY ACADEMIC
NEW YORK • LONDON • OXFORD • NEW DELHI • SYDNEY

BLOOMSBURY ACADEMIC
Bloomsbury Publishing Inc, 1385 Broadway, New York, NY 10018, USA
Bloomsbury Publishing Plc, 50 Bedford Square, London, WC1B 3DP, UK
Bloomsbury Publishing Ireland, 29 Earlsfort Terrace, Dublin 2, D02 AY28, Ireland

First published in the United States of America 2025

Cover design: Kathi Ha
Cover image © iStock/enjoynz

Library of Congress Cataloging-in-Publication Data

ISBN: HB: 978-1-5381-9830-8
PB: 978-1-5381-9831-5
epub: 978-1-5381-9832-2
epdf: 979-8-2163-6602-7

Typeset by Deanta Global Publishing Services, Chennai, India

Contents

Preface

The modern museum has more internal and external pressures than ever before. Navigating this ever-changing landscape requires a constant balancing act between competing priorities that always seem to be shifting. This book is intended for museum leaders who may not have all the necessary tools at their disposal to move their institution forward.

Sound financial management is a highly effective tool to help a museum to achieve its strategic priorities, enhance its decision-making apparatus, and deliver programs to its community. Financial management is a field as intricate as the art and artifacts that museums may house. It requires a level of financial literacy and a unique blend of skills and knowledge to effectively navigate the challenges and opportunities that will inevitably arise. To succeed long term, institutions must recognize that a shared financial responsibility is a critical enabler to mission priorities.

While the topic of this book is financial in nature, the audience of museum leaders is not limited to the museum's board, director, or chief financial officer. Assuming a museum's financial well-being rests only on this handful of positions is a recipe for failure. Leaders from across museum functions and levels have important roles to play. They are responsible for setting priorities for their area of responsibility, managing their resources, and getting ahead of potential pitfalls that could derail their plans. These responsibilities align with the disciplines of strategic planning, budgeting, and risk management. Leaders need not be the head of their institution's strategy, budget, or risk functions to understand the value of their application at the institutional, department, office, and team levels. Whether knowledge of these disciplines has been gained through formal professional education or inherently developed on the job, there can be no doubt that they are critical to each leader's success.

The Financial Integration and Resilience Model (FIRM) takes these disciplines to the next level by emphasizing the importance of building connections among them, rather than carrying them out as individual activities. Strategic planning and risk management must be established through their own robust processes with intentional links to the budgeting process through which all activities are resourced. FIRM further strengthens these connections by bringing attention to often neglected supporting capabilities of financial literacy, governance, change management, and financial tools. Museums that advance through FIRM become capable of complex, future-looking financial planning in the form of scenario planning and multi-year budgeting.

This book presents how each of these capabilities both stands on its own and provides the mutual support needed to establish long-term financial stability. The model organizes these topics based on their contribution toward a shared foundational knowledge and an internal infrastructure of integration and resilience. All the capabilities must work in harmony as a cohesive ecosystem or the financial infrastructure of a museum risks crumbling at its weakest points.

While some museum leaders reading this book may carry the institutional responsibilities of managing these individual processes, all readers benefit from understanding how these capabilities work together to enhance performance in their individual areas of responsibility. As we will discuss more in the change management chapter, for those whose institutions undertake advancements in any of FIRM's capabilities, leaders from throughout the institution enable success by stepping up to serve as champions and advocates of change.

The chapters that follow present the building blocks of FIRM through historical context and real-world museum challenges that may be similar to what readers are facing at their own museums. Practical hypotheticals from the perspectives of different museum roles and functions help the reader apply best practices and lessons learned to their own institution, regardless of the size or type of museum. Easy-to-understand tables and charts are used to guide readers through the application of FIRM.

The strength of the model lies in its flexibility and practicality. Not all museums will begin FIRM with the same level of financial literacy, the same endowment size, or the same capacity for advanced planning. Yet any museum can adapt its application of FIRM to its unique starting point. This book is intended to support the practical application of proven techniques to help the reader build connections across their financial ecosystem. The text is meant to be underlined, highlighted, and referred back to as a museum advances over time.

Part I

THE CURRENT STATE OF FINANCIAL MANAGEMENT

Chapter 1

Navigating Financial Uncertainty

Financial uncertainty is inherent in operating any museum. Sources of funding are becoming increasingly unreliable and operating costs continue to rise. Efforts to address these uncertainties often rest with the finance and development functions of the institution. The Financial Integration and Resilience Model, or FIRM, takes a different approach. FIRM asserts that only through institution-wide engagement and adaptability will a museum have the capacity to successfully navigate financial uncertainty. This chapter discusses the current financial challenges facing museums and introduces the elements of FIRM that will be explored throughout this book.

Museums are an integral part of the fabric of their communities. These institutions play a pivotal role in showcasing a community's history, fostering learning, and promoting a sense of collective identity. Museums house artifacts, artworks, and exhibits that allow visitors to feel as if they have traveled around the world or through time. By preserving, studying, and exhibiting these elements, museums become living archives that build connections across cultures and generations. This archival function helps communities maintain a sense of connection, understanding, and appreciation for the past, present, and future.

The pandemic highlighted the important role museums play in combating the growing problems of social isolation and loneliness. A 2023 advisory by the U.S. Surgeon General highlighted how strongly social connection and a sense of community are linked to physical and emotional health.[1] The advisory calls upon community-based organizations—like museums—to identify opportunities to foster connections within their community, build partnerships, promote public awareness, and generate social connections through their programming.[2]

Museums also play a critical role in filling the growing trust deficit. A 2021 survey found that museums rank high in trustworthiness among the public, second only to family and friends.[3] The survey found that museums are a more trusted source of information than the government, local and national news, and social media (which Americans rely on for information now more than ever). Even across diverse mission areas, zoos, art museums, science centers, and history museums were all held in similarly high esteem by those surveyed. In a world of partisan information, the survey confirms that museums are valued for their fact-based, objective neutrality, allowing visitors to draw their own conclusions about the information presented.

With museums being asked to fill all these critical roles in their communities, it is more essential than ever that a secure financial position enables them to keep their doors open and even extend their reach beyond their walls. Today, the relationship between museums and their communities is not limited to an in-person experience. Museums are constantly evolving and rethinking how they interact with their visitors. Content and information are being incorporated, accessed, and evaluated through multiple types of media and experiences.

Museums are working hard to keep pace with a dynamic world and avoid becoming static enterprises that only exist behind inaccessible glass dividers. Recent survey data indicates that 99 percent of nonprofits said they meaningfully expanded or shifted the scope of their mission in the past 12 months and 42 percent indicated that they will be undergoing a digital transformation.[4]

As audiences demand new ways to engage with collections, museums are planning for how to adapt. In 2024, 129 years after opening its doors for the first time, the Brooklyn Museum in New York completed a $50-million renovation complete with state-of-the-art audiovisual and lighting capabilities.[5] The renovation is part of the institution's effort to better connect with intergenerational groups through interactive programming.[6]

Digital transformations require an influx of financial resources, are very time-consuming, and generate higher back-end information technology costs. A museum should not take for granted that once the funds have been raised the institution's ecosystem can support a major renovation seamlessly, especially if it struggles with financial literacy.

Recent years have highlighted how unforeseen events can dramatically challenge museum operations and the ability to deliver information, programs, and content for their respective communities. During the pandemic, many museums were unprepared for the hybrid programming and asynchronous learning tools needed to continue reaching their audiences safely. They did not have the educational material and technology to quickly adapt to this new way of delivering programs.

The speed of change can overtake an institution's ability to manage this unstable landscape and hinder its goals to expand its mission and reach broader audiences. Museum leadership must ask themselves if they have the internal structures in place to make this expansion achievable and sustainable. How do they carry out this growth in the face of funding uncertainty and rising costs?

FUNDING UNCERTAINTY

The key external financial risk to museums is the reduction of government funding or philanthropic support. Funding uncertainty can cause a museum's financial stability to vary dramatically from year to year. Without sufficient funding, a museum cannot achieve planned growth, is forced to put projects or initiatives on hold, or may even need to make cuts to current operations.

In the worst-case scenario, a museum may close their doors because it cannot navigate the financial landscape. The Rubin Museum of Art in Manhattan, home to art from Himalayan Asia, was forced to sell its facility in 2024 due in part to funding challenges.[7] With no physical building and major staffing cuts, the Rubin is being reimagined as a museum without walls focused on long-term loans and traveling exhibits.[8] Elevating financial management to a core value can ensure that the focus on the collection is not disconnected from the museum's long-term financial health.

The lack of a particular type of funding may have an outsized impact on museum operations and future plans if other sources cannot substitute for the need. New York's Metropolitan Museum of Art recently replenished its acquisition fund with the proceeds from the sale of multiple items from their collection, including a portrait of George Washington which sold for $2.8 million.[9] Long-term financial planning and scenario planning, which we will discuss in future chapters, are the difference between selling parts of the collection as a last resort or a well-planned strategy to ensure long-term stability.

Fundraising is an increasingly competitive field, leading museums to begin developing strategies to ensure that they have multiple revenue streams for their financial health and stability. 24 percent of the revenue that U.S. museums receive comes from public partners.[10] Collaboration between a museum and government entities at the national, state, or municipal level can be a significant enabler of museum operations. The purpose of the funding may be general support to the museum's mission or for specific exhibits, projects, or programs.

The public–private partnership between the U.S. government and the Smithsonian Institution provides more than $1 billion a year to support its operating budget and facility improvements.[11] This government investment drastically reduces the Smithsonian's reliance on endowment, private contributions, and earned revenue sources such as retail sales and concessions. This partnership also allows the Smithsonian Institution to forgo an admission fee for its visitors, ensuring maximum accessibility by the public. Outside of major cities with significant tourism, only about 10 percent of a museum's operating expenses can be offset with ticket sales.[12] To the extent the institution's budget relies on required or recommended entrance fees, a decline in attendance can be a critical financial risk factor. Lower attendance also leads to reduced revenue from retail and concessions.

The Smithsonian operating model includes public support for basic operations and facility needs, while the institution must raise private funds to support its academic and public engagement pursuits. New York City has provided funds to maintain and secure the facility and grounds of the Museum of Natural History for more than 150 years.[13] Private funds are raised for programming, research, collections, and other work pursued by the museum.[14] However, the museum has publicly expressed concerns regarding city budget proposals that cut the Department of Cultural Affairs from which it receives public funds.[15]

Working with public partners has become so critical to museum leadership that the American Alliance of Museums (AAM) organizes an annual Museums Advocacy Day.[16] Alliance members gather in Washington, D.C., each year to walk the halls of Congress to emphasize to lawmakers the value and importance of investing public resources in museums.[17] AAM provides its members with guides on how to "Advocate from Anywhere," employing similar strategies to influence current and potential public partners at all levels of government.[18] Museums work collectively at the local level as well, such as through the Cultural Institutions Group that represents over thirty New York City area museums in their public–private partnerships with state and city governments.[19]

Public funds can be a critical lifeline when facing unexpected financial challenges. With the help of the U.S. Congress, the National Endowment for the Arts and the National Endowment for the Humanities each received $162.2 million in 2020 to support museums navigating the uncertainty of the pandemic.[20] The federal stimulus bill known as the CARES Act also made available another $300 million in pandemic support.[21]

In one notable example, the intersection between public and private funding has actually prevented the use of public funds already secured. The Morris Jumel Mansion secured over $5 million from the New York City parks department to repair the historic house's deteriorating exterior, but the city government will not allow the funds to be spent until the remainder of the rehabilitation project costs can be raised with private funds.[22] Juggling multiple funding sources requires financial management tools to manage project timelines, fundraising campaigns, and relationships with federal and state partners so projects are always moving forward.

Public funding uncertainty can stem from a variety of causes. Government-wide budget cuts, de-prioritization of arts and culture investment, or the politics surrounding a particular institution's mission or programming can all lead to a loss of public funding. A museum's ability to advocate against such reductions can depend on how much notice the museum is given and its level of influence with government officials. In 2024, the Florida governor cut $32 million from the state's arts and culture budget, citing disagreement with using state funds for a festival that would have received just $7,000 in grant money.[23] Hundreds of diverse organizations including museums, galleries, zoos, dance companies, and community theaters were impacted across the state.[24] Other reductions to public funds are relative, as they simply fail to keep pace with inflating operating costs. Regardless of the reason, the lack of sufficient public funding forces a museum to either fill the gap with additional private funding or make internal cuts.

Creative ideas to sidestep politics and enable steady sources of public funding are coming to the forefront. In 2012, three counties in Michigan voted to establish a property tax in support of the Detroit Institute of Arts (DIA).[25] The ten-year plan, which was extended in 2020, was designed to help support DIA's operational costs while the institution focused on growing its endowment.[26] The goal was to achieve an endowment payout sufficient to support DIA by the time the tax sunsets.[27] Direct taxpayer support carries a high expectation of accountability and return on investment. DIA is required to annually demonstrate how it uses the funds to provide benefits to the local community, such as free museum admission, transportation for school field trips and senior groups, teacher workshops, and community partnerships.[28] The DIA model has faced some public criticism, arguing that too much of the funds have gone to operating costs rather than expanding programming and community engagement.[29]

A bold proposal from some nonprofit leaders argues that the government mindset regarding arts and cultural institutions should shift from luxury to infrastructure.[30] This proposal places museums on par with investments like highways and utilities by focusing funding on core operations of museum buildings. The proposal's approach is in contrast to the current grant model of funding specific exhibits or initiatives that can become mired in controversy over their content. The proposal recognizes the economic force of arts and culture institutions in local economies as employers and tourist destinations.

Seeking funds from private donors and foundations comes with a different set of challenges. Charitable giving from Americans fell 6.4 percent from 2021 to 2023.[31] Adjusted for inflation, this represented a decline of $10.5 million in total giving.[32] In a recent survey of nonprofits, 36 percent of respondents indicated that they are seeking new revenue sources.[33] Museums can no longer count on an upward trajectory in fundraising.

All private funding is not created equal. Contributions have a different impact on museum operations depending on whether the funds can be spent directly or if the donor wants to invest the funds in an endowment. Building an endowment is a long-term financial commitment that can feel like a hindrance to immediate financial needs. A museum may raise millions of dollars for the endowment and find that staff struggle to understand why none of these funds can be applied to their programs and projects. It may take a generation for a museum to grow its endowment into a revenue stream that can be relied on for stable and predictable payouts.

Museums that have come to expect endowment payouts as one of their funding sources face the additional challenge of market turbulence. The value of endowment investments can experience significant fluctuations, affecting the overall value of the endowment. This volatility introduces uncertainty and poses challenges for institutions that depend on the endowment's returns to fund operational expenses, exhibits, research initiatives, and other commitments. Market downturns can trigger a reduction in the endowment's value, subsequently affecting the funds available for distribution. Inflation is also an enemy of the endowment, offsetting market gains in the endowment with increased costs.

Donor restrictions can have a significant impact on endowments, influencing their ability to fulfill their intended purposes. A 2020 survey indicated that 61 percent of endowments are permanently restricted, 20 percent are temporarily restricted, and 19 percent are unrestricted.[34] Museum leaders need to ensure that their use of the funds does not violate the terms and conditions of each gift, while at the same time considering how the various restrictions impact the museum's ability to adequately resource its strategic goals.

Even those gifts that are available to spend can be complicated by donors choosing to place restrictions on their use. A restricted gift may limit the use of funds to a particular exhibit, program, named position, or other purpose. Museums may find that they are unable to fully execute the funds if the purpose is overly restrictive or the program's needs have changed. A large restricted gift may provide five years of funding for Project A, while Project B is underfunded and forced to make cuts. Furthermore, the museum must determine what happens to Project A after the restricted gift that supported it is fully spent.

With all these challenges, it's no wonder that museums prefer to raise funds without restrictions. At the same time, discerning donors are often experienced investors who want to know the impact of their donation or support a specific area that may have personal meaning to them. These competing factors require careful balancing by fundraising teams and museum leadership. A restricted gift may be preferable to the risk that a donor takes their money elsewhere.

The more restricted gifts and endowments a museum receives, the more complicated program execution becomes. These funds require close monitoring and reporting back to donors on how they were used. The additional workload associated with managing restricted funds can create additional overhead costs that may or may not be covered by the terms and conditions of the restriction.

RISING COSTS

Even a well-resourced institution can face financial uncertainty posed by changing economic conditions. Rising inflation can frighten away potential donors, reduce visitorship, and increase operating costs. Even moderate inflation can lead to increased expenses across museum offices and impact the institution's overall budgetary needs. Simply put, the same amount of funds will not stretch as far as they did from one year to the next.

The reality is that ongoing costs that keep museum buildings operating—such as maintenance, utilities, and staff—make up a substantial percentage of a museum's total budget. These costs are not visible to the average visitor, except perhaps in their absence when a visitor eyes a bucket catching drips from a leaky roof, an out of service sign on the elevator, or an unattended visitor services desk. But these core operational costs are foundational to the visitor experience and programming investments that are layered on top of them. This lack of visibility is the same reason private donors may be uninterested in underwriting these costs and why government grant rules often exclude them.

Inflation drives up prices for goods and services needed to maintain museum facilities, design new exhibits, and sustain educational programs. Contract service providers will pass along increased costs of doing business. Museum employees may seek other employment opportunities unless their salaries keep pace with the rising cost of living. As utility and maintenance costs continue to rise, some museums are looking to clean energy grants to make big investments now, which can reduce these ever-inflating costs in future years.

Support functions such as information technology can be difficult fundraising propositions and often rely on public or unrestricted funds. Cybersecurity impacts both the overall budget of a museum and the accessibility and safety of the collection. About 59 percent of nonprofits reported that they are increasing technology spending and 95 percent say they are concerned about cyberattacks.[35] Not all cyberattacks are publicly known, and some are more costly than others. One case reported in January 2024 involved a cyberattack targeting a collection- and archive-management software used by many U.S. arts institutions.[36] The attack rendered digital collections displays temporarily inaccessible, hindering museum operations.[37]

The cost of IT professionals, security software, and incident monitoring tools will continue to rise in cost over time, requiring ongoing training, maintenance, and product upgrades. IT costs are going up as much as 8 percent a year, a significant increase to a museum's budget for a function that is not public-facing.[38]

Disruptions are not limited to cyber incidents. As high-profile institutions within their community, museums can find themselves the target of damaging or dangerous real-world activity. Climate activists have damaged or attempted to damage works of art all over the world. The Mona Lisa has been a constant target for environmental protests.[39] In 2009, a white supremacist opened fire at the U.S. Holocaust Memorial Museum, killing a special police officer.[40] These incidents make investments in physical security just as important as cybersecurity and another area of ever-rising cost.

Unanticipated government mandates can also create new and in some cases unplanned operational expenses. In 2024, federal regulations established more stringent rules around the study or display of Native human remains and cultural objects without proper consent.[41] Museums like the American Museum of Natural History in New York immediately closed galleries housing such objects while they determine if they can meet this stricter standard.[42] Museums will incur unanticipated costs to ensure compliance with the regulation and determine how best to ensure protection of Native rights in the storytelling of future exhibits.

A common response to rising costs is to increase ticket prices or reduce operating hours. Both actions diminish a museum's core value of accessibility. In 2023, multiple U.S. museums made difficult decisions to address rising costs.[43] The Guggenheim Museum in New York raised ticket prices and laid off ten workers.[44] The San Francisco Museum of Modern Art eliminated twenty staff positions, citing a 35 percent drop in attendance from 2019.[45] The Dallas Museum of Art cut twenty employees and reduced the number of days it is open to the public each week.[46] Programming and community services are often the first to go as limited resources are focused on maintaining core operations. Layoffs, programming cuts, collection sell-off, building closures, and debt are all too common for museums struggling to make ends meet. Financially unstable museums may need to make multiple rounds of difficult cuts while at the same time doing all they can to secure more funds.

THE SEARCH FOR SOLUTIONS

Funding uncertainty coupled with rising costs can conjure a daunting future for museum leaders. These factors are forcing museums to begin making difficult decisions that affect their long-term viability. Some museums that feel secure in their near-term financial footing may not yet feel the full weight of these growing risks and put them off as a future problem. Others may try specific tactics to plan for the future.

Traditional solutions used across the spectrum of government agencies, museums, universities, and foundations address these challenges in the same fundamental manner. Budget cuts are often the first action in the face of financial uncertainty. Building a strategic plan is a common exercise when an organization wants to clarify its mission and attract funding. A 2023 survey found that 57 percent of nonprofits plan to invest in enterprise resource planning tools to help them with financial decision-making.[47] In isolation, actions like these will have some financial impact, but are not sufficient to enable long-term financial health. They also can have unintended internal consequences, increasing a sense of resource competition within the institution and entrenching siloed thinking as programs jockey to be seen as higher priorities.

Too often, these solutions are taken on by individual offices. A museum's fundraising staff prepares new fundraising approaches, the finance office looks for cost-cutting opportunities, and programs consider what work to prioritize. Too often, these solutions are abandoned when the problem at hand is addressed, and the institution returns to business as usual without the foundation needed to face challenges on the horizon and ensure long-term financial stability.

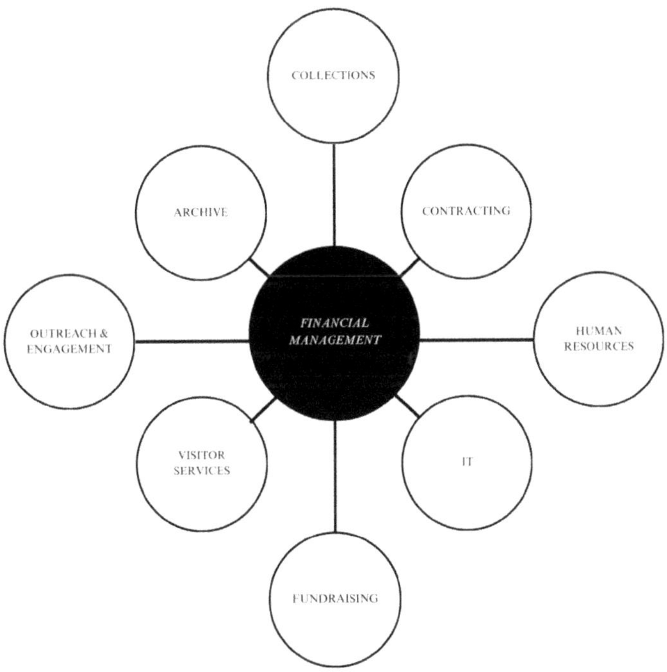

Figure 1.1 Financial Management Touchpoints throughout a Museum. *Source*: Ashley Amos.

All of the real-world examples cited in this chapter—and the many more that can be found in the news in recent years—point to a common theme. Museums are uniquely challenged by complex financial structures and uniquely visible in their communities when something goes wrong. It is impossible for anyone outside of the leaders of these museums to know exactly what has happened and what could have been done to prevent it. No museum wants to find itself in the situation in which making drastic cuts or selling off of assets is the only way to survive. It is incumbent on all museum leaders to institute comprehensive approaches to bolster their financial management.

THE FINANCIAL INTEGRATION AND RESILIENCE MODEL

The modern museum requires a robust financial management model that can adapt to our rapidly changing world. Financial health and stability are enablers of mission-driven institutions, and they can be inhibitors if not actively maintained. Museum missions are

Figure 1.2 Disjointed (Top) and Collaborative (Bottom) Mission Execution. *Source*: Ashley Amos.

traditionally viewed through the lens of programmatic work, and the finance function is considered essential only to the extent that it ensures the funds are available to make those programs run smoothly. Further, the finance office is often considered an operational or support element, responsible for daily actions like processing revenue and paying bills, not a strategic partner.

FIRM elevates a museum's financial management to a strategic priority and core value. FIRM coalesces what may currently be disparate actions around the recognition that finance is not just one office in the museum but an ecosystem that intersects every part of the institution. Financial issues flow through so many other functions of the institution, from fundraising, to staffing, to long-range planning. Institution-wide financial processes can build connection points with the work of other offices that can be mutually beneficial and ensure that everyone is working in the same direction.

The elevation of financial management does not diminish the importance of other values or priorities held by the institution, but rather ensures the success of these endeavors because they are not detached from resource planning. This shift means more than just giving the finance office a seat at the decision-making table. A fully realized financial management function underpins strategic decision-making and contributes to overall organizational stability. Under FIRM, museum leaders engage the entire institution in difficult discussions and leverage an array of tools to inform institutional decisions.

FIRM begins with Financial Literacy as the foundation. Atop this foundation sit the twin pillars of Integration and Resilience, two principles that must be woven into the fabric of an institution to foster financial health and stability. Only an integrated institution will have the resilience to weather an unforeseen event. The first pillar, Integration, ensures that the museum operates as one cohesive body and involves all stakeholders in making financially informed decisions. The second pillar, Resilience, ensures that the tools are in place to adapt to a changing world. One pillar cannot stand without the other, and each consists of building blocks that put these principles into action to strengthen museum operations.

Figure 1.3 The Financial Integration and Resilience Model. *Source*: Ashley Amos.

Foundation: Financial Literacy

Financial Literacy refers to the shared set of financial language, processes, and competencies that are leveraged within an institution. Employees at all levels must have the appropriate level of financial literacy to carry out their responsibilities consistently and with clear communication across roles. Financial literacy provides an essential baseline for building an institution-wide financial capability.

Pillar One: Integration

Organizations of all types develop silos that limit engagement across boundaries. Lack of information sharing, poor and fragmented communication, and disparate planning structures can all contribute to the inability to share and integrate data across an organization. One of the most famous and well-documented cases of siloed operations was among U.S. forces in the days leading up to the Japanese attack on Pearl Harbor in 1941.[48] Failure to share information and respond to warning signs left the Pacific naval base unprepared and thrust America into World War II.[49] A museum that is not actively engaging across all of its operational and programmatic offices will find that both large and small matters become harder to plan for and respond to in an organized manner. Perhaps the facilities team does not inform the museum's curators that the museum will be without its HVAC system, and no one considers artifacts that require stable environmental conditions.

Museum offices spend most of their time focused on their day-to-day work and to some extent their long-term plans. Staff may have limited interaction with other offices outside of joint projects. Programmatic offices reach out to support offices like finance, legal, and human resources when specific help is needed. Offices go directly to museum leadership to advocate for their needs and priorities. Leadership at the top holds all the decision-making authority for each individual silo.

A siloed institution creates a culture of discord, secrecy, and competition for resources. Two offices may separately meet with the museum director to discuss a project that needs an additional $10,000 in funding. Neither office knows that they are in direct competition with the other, but both know that resources are limited. Unless the museum director happens to have $20,000 available to give, they cannot say yes to both offices. The decision to say yes to one request is a tacit decision to say no to the other. Allocating the $10,000 now also means that the director must say no to future requests by other offices that may arise later in the year.

When the director relays their decision to both requesting offices, they may not choose to disclose that two requests were made. After all, the office that was told no may be upset that another office's work was chosen over theirs. The director may ask the successful office to keep the decision between them so as not to spark jealousy from other offices. This decision-making approach creates an unhealthy dynamic and a distrustful culture.

Open communication and transparent decision-making are hallmarks of an integrated institution. Integration promotes collaboration, consistency, and efficiency. An integrated institution seeks to build connections and shared understanding across offices. Offices are encouraged to see their work in relation to the broader mission. Museum leadership trust offices with the knowledge of institutional decisions and the trade-offs that must be made. Most importantly, integration enables the swift, enterprise-level decisions needed to respond to changing financial conditions.

FIRM's Integration pillar includes four building blocks: Budgeting, Strategic Planning, Governance, and Change Management.

Budgeting is the annual effort to prepare, resource, and carry out a spending plan. It involves matching the financial resources that are available or expected to be available with estimated costs of personnel, goods, and services for the upcoming year.

Strategic Planning is a process that a museum uses to define its direction and pursue specific objectives. It involves setting goals, assessing the current state, identifying opportunities and challenges, and developing strategies to achieve long-term success. Strategic planning provides a roadmap for institutions to align their actions and resources with their mission and vision.

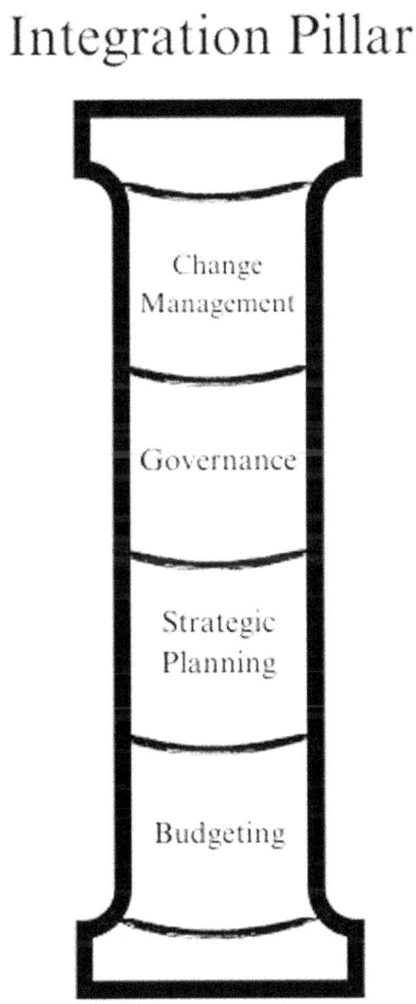

Figure 1.4 Building Blocks of the Integration Pillar. *Source*: Ashley Amos.

Governance refers to the rules, roles, and responsibilities put in place for effective organizational management. Governance creates transparent and accountable structures that consider all stakeholders while adopting an institution-wide perspective.

Change Management is the structured approach used to transition individuals, teams, or entire institutions from the current state to a desired future state. It involves planning, implementing, and reinforcing changes to achieve organizational goals. Effective change management addresses employee concerns and leverages communication strategies to ensure a smooth transition, reducing resistance and increasing the chances of successful change implementation.

Pillar Two: Resilience

Resilience is a museum's ability to anticipate and respond to financial adversity and challenges. A resilient institution employs various monitoring, planning, and analysis tools to fortify itself against uncertainties. With a better understanding of the world around it, the institution is better positioned to thrive in a dynamic environment.

Financial resilience cannot exist without integration, which enables an institution to respond to the changing conditions in a systematic and cohesive manner. To understand how FIRM's two pillars work hand-in-hand, let us return to the example of the two offices asking their director for $10,000. An integrated institution will provide a forum for these new budget needs to be considered. Each office will produce a standardized justification for the funding request, including its cost assumptions, its impact on the larger project, and how it will advance the museum's strategic goals. After hearing from all requesters, members of the forum will reach consensus and communicate the outcome to all parties. This is how an integrated institution handles the unexpected.

But how do the decision-makers know what factors to weigh in their decision? The forum may review budget execution data to see if $10,000 is available for approval. The latest budget may show that another project has recently reduced its planned expenses by $15,000, providing enough funds to meet at least one request. If sufficient funds are not currently available, the decision-makers could consult the latest fundraising projections to understand if more resources are likely to be available soon and weigh the near- and mid-term risks of delaying the project until funds arrive. A resilient institution has these tools and more at their disposal to help them see all the pathways available to them and inform their decisions.

FIRM's resilience pillar includes four building blocks that together provide a museum with strategic foresight: Risk Management, Financial Tools, Scenario Planning, and Multi-year Budgeting.

Risk Management is the process of identifying, assessing, and prioritizing potential risks or uncertainties that may affect the achievement of museum objectives. It involves analyzing the potential impact of these risks and implementing strategies to manage them effectively. The goal of risk management is to minimize the negative impacts of uncertainties while maximizing opportunities for the institution. A resilient museum will have an entity-wide risk register that includes risk management strategies and risk indicators that are tracked and measured over time.

Financial Tools encompass a range of software and models designed to manage and streamline financial processes within an organization. Effective use of financial tools enhances accuracy, efficiency, and foresight in financial operations, contributing to better decision-making and overall financial health for organizations.

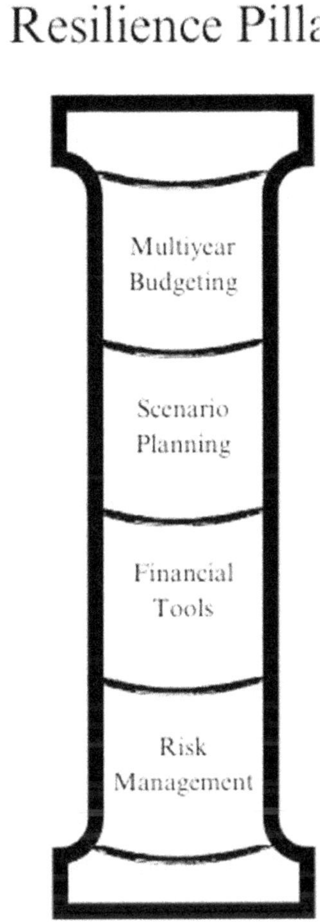

Figure 1.5 Building Blocks of the Resilience Pillar. *Source*: Ashley Amos.

Scenario Planning involves creating and analyzing possible future scenarios to anticipate and prepare for uncertainties. A museum that uses this approach considers various potential developments, disruptions, or changes in their environment. By developing multiple positive and negative scenarios, a museum can explore different future conditions and assess how it would perform under each scenario. This proactive approach helps organizations to be more adaptable, making informed decisions that consider a range of possible futures rather than relying on a single forecast.

Multi-year Budgeting is a financial planning approach where high-level budgets are developed and approved for a period exceeding one budget year. Instead of focusing solely on the upcoming year, a museum will use multi-year budgeting to plan for an extended time frame, often spanning two to five years. This approach allows for a more strategic and comprehensive financial outlook, enabling the institution to align its budget activity with the long-term goals and priorities of its strategic plan. It provides a framework for improved resource allocation, investment planning, and overall financial sustainability.

The FIRM Self-Assessment

FIRM aligns a suite of capabilities to improve financial health and long-term stability. Many of these ingredients for success are already being carried out within institutions and are familiar to museum leaders. However, their impact can be narrow and short-lived if not practiced in concert and across the institution. Achieving FIRM's comprehensive approach to financial management requires museum leadership to advance existing practices across all the FIRM building blocks to form an integrated and resilient financial ecosystem.

Each museum will have a different starting point, with some of the building blocks in place with varying degrees of complexity and connectivity. The FIRM self-assessment tool enables each reader to better understand their unique starting point. The self-assessment asks the reader to evaluate how well they carry out the capabilities of FIRM's eight building blocks. Because financial literacy is foundational to full execution of all the building blocks, readers rate the execution of each capability as demonstrating a basic, intermediate, or advanced level of financial literacy. The scale also includes the "no capability" selection for building blocks that the reader does not consider formalized at any level in their institution.

The role of the reader in their museum can alter the level of evaluation in the self-assessment. A museum director will naturally consider the whole institution in their assessment. An office head may complete the template keeping in mind the business practices of only their area of responsibility. It may be valuable to have multiple executives undertake a museum-wide

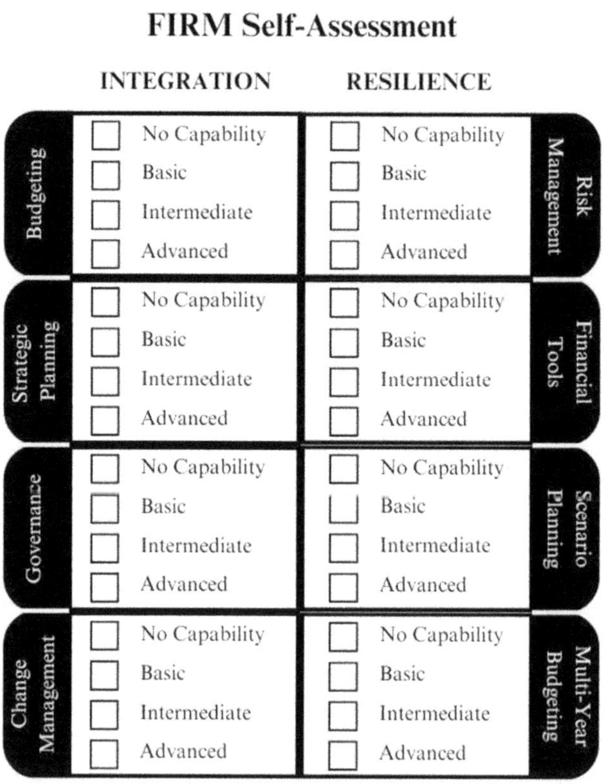

Figure 1.6 FIRM Self-assessment. *Source*: Ashley Amos.

assessment to understand if they hold varying perspectives on the current state of these capabilities. Areas of misalignment in assessment results can stimulate valuable discussion. Perhaps the chief financial officer considers the budgeting capability to be advanced, but the museum operations executive selects the low option. Further exploration may reveal variable levels of financial literacy across the institution in which some offices lack the skills and support they need to effectively participate in the established budget process.

The self-assessment can be taken now or after reading the chapter on financial literacy. While basic, intermediate, and advanced are relatively self-evident terms, the next chapter provides greater context on how the reader can differentiate between these levels in describing financial skills and knowledge. A shared baseline of terminology—as we will discuss in the financial literacy chapter—is particularly valuable when a group of museum leaders are completing their own assessments and comparing results. For instance, "advanced" strategic planning in the context of FIRM does not just mean that an institution is very good at developing a strategic plan every planning cycle. Rather, the museum must have a robust strategic planning process that enables ongoing strategic decision-making and is formally linked to the budgeting process.

The financial literacy chapter provides a primer that will be further elaborated on when applied to each building block. The chapters that follow will explore FIRM in greater depth by breaking down each building block and providing insights into how they can be undertaken and tied together. The self-assessment will appear again at the end of the book to enable the reader to examine how the teachings of FIRM have altered their view of their current state. The self-assessment can then be used as an ongoing monitoring tool as an institution progresses in its FIRM journey.

Part II

THE FOUNDATION

Chapter 2

Financial Literacy

FIRM establishes financial literacy as foundational to improving the financial health and stability of an institution. Continual advancement of financial literacy is the enabler of each of FIRM's building blocks. It is important to keep in mind that every institution will start with its own level of financial literacy that must be assessed and understood before undertaking efforts to build its financial ecosystem.

Financial literacy is a term primarily used in the context of personal finance. It includes the basic skills a person needs to pay their bills, save money for vacations or college funds, and plan for retirement. However, personal financial literacy does not necessarily translate to the financial knowledge needed in a professional context.

Most professionals who interact with the financial ecosystem of their workplace don't need degrees in finance, but it is unreasonable for an institution to assume that an employee's personal financial literacy is sufficient for their success. Institutional finances are infinitely more complex than personal finances, involving numerous funding sources that must be shared across multiple users. Interacting with an institution's financial realm requires a different type of financial literacy.

Museum leaders can examine financial literacy through two lenses: individual and institutional. Individual financial literacy considers whether each employee possesses the skills, knowledge, and abilities to effectively carry out the financial aspects of their job. Institutional financial literacy looks at the museum as a whole. An institution advances its financial literacy by implementing more sophisticated and interrelated financial processes and tools. Such an institution must ensure that individual financial literacy does not fall behind these advances. Otherwise, employees tasked with implementing these processes and using these tools may not know how to do what is expected of them. The two types of financial literacy must advance in tandem: a museum that is implementing more advanced financial processes and tools must take into account where its employees may be starting from and how quickly they can learn new skills.

The inverse scenario is also problematic. Employees with a high degree of individual financial literacy may be frustrated by outdated processes and insufficient tools. Perhaps they honed their financial skills and training at another institution that had these capabilities and now feel they are unable to carry out their work as effectively without them. They may resort to more tedious manual efforts to collect and track data in the absence of support. In this case, the museum needs to examine its current ways of doing business to ensure institutional financial literacy is keeping pace.

In the real world, literacy levels are not simply high or low across the board. Some employees may be more capable than others, and some processes and tools may have been updated more recently than others. Museum leaders will need to find the balance between these two types of literacy in each case. More advanced employees can be a valuable source of best practices that can be adopted as new processes and tools. Less advanced employees can be a litmus test to see if proposed improvements can be learned and adopted.

INDIVIDUAL FINANCIAL LITERACY

Individual financial literacy goes beyond a museum professional's ability to do math. This type of financial literacy requires that all employees know where they fit into the financial ecosystem and possess the language and capabilities that enable them to interact with, interpret, and act on financial information.

There are many areas outside an employee's core job description that museum leadership expects them to understand. All organizations ensure their staff are regularly trained on a variety of non-programmatic priorities, like cyber hygiene, harassment and discrimination, and records retention. However, financial literacy in nonfinancial positions is often expected to be self-taught or learned on the job. Too often, position descriptions and hiring announcements fail to mention that the incumbent has some financial duties or is expected to have certain financial competencies.

Every employee of a museum likely needs to possess some degree of financial literacy. The level of financial literacy varies from position to position and from individual to individual. An office head does not need to know the details of how an administrative assistant in their office manages a contract or processes an invoice. Rather, the office head is expected to understand their office's total budget and how it is carried out to achieve their priorities. Likewise, the administrative assistant is not charged with making strategic decisions regarding the office's budget. Rather, the administrative assistant is expected to follow protocols for monitoring contract performance and paying the invoices on a timely basis.

Gaps in individual financial literacy occur when employees do not fully understand how finance intersects with their role. These differences in understanding or ways of carrying out work will prevent smooth financial management, which in turn prevents the optimization of museum resources toward its strategic goals.

Consider the impact if our hypothetical administrative assistant wasn't closely monitoring a contractor's performance as it exceeded the amount budgeted for the contract. Or the assistant isn't comfortable with the museum's electronic routing procedures for invoice approval so they walk around the office to collect signatures like they did at their last job. Perhaps our hypothetical office head does not prioritize tracking their budget because they are focused on their area of scholarship.

Worse still, imagine if these two people work together. The administrative assistant may be racking up cost overruns and incurring costly late fees that put the contract at risk. Meanwhile, the office head may not notice an issue until the additional costs overtake other budget needs or the vendor stops its work. The lack of financial literacy leads to problems that take significantly more time to untangle after the fact than it would have taken to learn the necessary financial skills in advance.

Financial Language Barriers

A common hindrance to individual financial literacy is a lack of shared financial language. An employee in the finance office may speak to an employee in a programmatic area using unfamiliar financial jargon. The information conveyed may be valuable, but have an unclear meaning and may result in the information being lost in translation.

There are estimated to be 7,000 languages spoken around the world and over 300 languages spoken in the United States.[1] Significant time and resources are lost when people cannot communicate effectively because they speak different languages—or even different dialects of the same language. Understanding financial terminology can feel a lot like learning a foreign language. Museum professionals are experts in their fields with advanced degrees in numerous disciplines, but their experience with financial matters may draw from managing their personal finances or financial approaches used in other institutions at which they have worked. Adopting and promulgating a shared financial language is essential to ensure that everyone has a strong baseline for financial literacy.

Financial language should be established based on industry standards. However, similar to dialects, not every industry has the same standards. For example, budget is a commonly used term across all organizations, but a budget can look very different whether it is a government budget, a corporate budget, or a museum budget. There are also various budgeting approaches that have their own terms: a cash budget is built using only the funds in hand; a zero-based budget makes spending decisions from the ground up each year. These terms are not interchangeable and can cause confusion if institutions are not intentional in selecting the language that best meets their needs.

In the spirit of building shared financial language, key terms used throughout this book are defined to provide readers with a shared understanding of their meaning. Similarly, all institutions should adopt their own set of definitions to incorporate into their training and daily activities. Definitions may need to be adapted to specific environments or expanded upon with additional detail based on each museum's unique needs.

INSTITUTIONAL FINANCIAL LITERACY

Financial literacy can also be viewed through the lens of the institution. Institutional financial literacy extends beyond the staff performing the operational and tactical actions at a museum. The consequences of poor institutional financial literacy are much more impactful and severe than poor individual financial literacy because the gaps don't rest with a single employee—they affect the financial performance of the institution as a whole.

The Bellevue Arts Museum in Washington opened its first permanent location in 2000; however, the founders did not establish a large enough endowment to eventually contribute to operating costs.[2] This gap in financial planning increased the museum's reliance on annual fundraising efforts.[3] By 2024, the museum found itself operating at a deficit and announced a capital campaign to help cover operating costs and outstanding debt.[4] As the campaign progresses, the museum will need to balance immediate funding needs with the long-term benefit of growing the endowment. Individual donors may have differing preferences on which to support, and they may not have the giving capacity to fully meet both needs. As museums consider their future, financial literacy means not just planning for one year, but planning for the museum's long-term future.

Financial literacy also ensures that a museum considers the totality of its actions and understands that they may have a cascading effect on its future sustainability. In 2006, the Milwaukee Public Museum was over $40 million in debt and had a budget deficit; its endowment value was under $400,000.[5] The museum had overspent on an expansion plan and borrowed significant funds to support investments such as IMAX theaters, a rainforest in Costa Rica, and a string of statewide museum shops.[6] The museum drastically reduced its staff, began the process of restructuring its debt, and significantly increased its fundraising.[7] By 2024, the museum had turned the corner, having raised enough funds to break ground on a new facility with a smaller footprint augmented by offsite storage of the remainder of their collection.[8]

For decades, the Corcoran Gallery of Art in Washington, D.C., was showing symptoms of poor institutional financial literacy: it was struggling to remain competitive in a city awash with museums and had a poorly maintained 130-year-old historic building with skyrocketing capital costs.[9] Leaders sought to compete with its federally subsidized neighbors with a $17-million design for a flashy new facility with estimated construction costs of $160 million.[10] A series of economic downturns and other external events stalled the capital campaign for the construction, and the worsening financial position of the institution became unsalvageable.[11] The Corcoran was sold to George Washington University in 2014.[12] The university provided the funds needed to maintain the historical building, and the costly architectural design was never used.[13]

While we now have the benefit of hindsight, examples like these prompt the question of whether the museums had sufficient institutional financial literacy to enable informed decision-making.

Growing financial literacy for an entire institution involves adopting increasingly sophisticated financial management processes and tools. Financial literacy is incremental, but can be broken down into three levels. The typical capabilities of institutions at these levels are described to illustrate how advancing financial literacy can create the financial health and stability that enables continued operation for many years to come.

Basic Level

A museum with a basic level of financial literacy may only be executing the first few building blocks of FIRM. Nearly every institution undergoes some form of annual budgeting process. At the basic level, the budget process may involve simple manual estimations in a spreadsheet. Most institutions have undergone the exercise of preparing a strategic plan at some point, though it may be in need of a refresh. A museum with basic financial literacy may leverage the strategic plan goals for external messaging to donors and other stakeholders, but struggle to connect the long-term aspirations of the strategic plan to annual budget decisions.

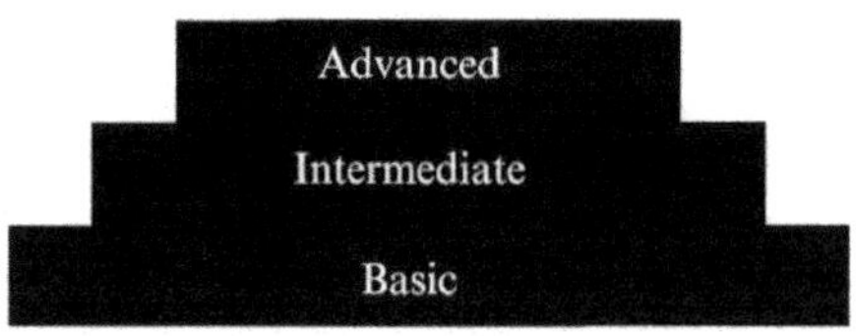

Figure 2.1 Levels of Financial Literacy. *Source*: Ashley Amos.

A museum with basic financial literacy will find that it spends much of its time reacting to events as they happen. Such an institution may observe financial market fluctuations but does not have a plan in place to weather a short-term financial disruption. Museum leaders are assembled quickly as problems arise, but they lack the tools to predict or mitigate these problems. Office heads and managers may operate without a clear sense of what resources may be available to them in the future, causing them to retreat to their silos and hold onto any money they can.

Perhaps a museum's development office has been highly successful in garnering donations for one program while the finance office struggles to fund other strategic priorities in next year's budget. The museum may have accumulated numerous restricted funding sources that no longer align with program needs and cannot be spent. Museum leaders may have trouble squaring reports from development that fundraising has been successful with concerns from the finance office about unspent balances and from programs about insufficient funds to support their work. Lacking the processes and tools to bring this differing perspectives together to a single financial picture, the museum may continue its path unchanged until the funding situation becomes dire.

Intermediate Level

A museum with an intermediate level of financial literacy is undertaking efforts to bolster and connect the basic building blocks of FIRM. Consulting its financial systems and tools, a museum may inform its budget process with an analysis of historical spending trends. Difficult budget decisions can be elevated to a governing body responsible for aligning spending with the institution's strategic goals.

At the intermediate level, an institution is decreasing reliance on manual processes with a high risk of human error, instead building more system-based or automated processes. These improved processes provide valuable resources for employees to consult without significant work time.

For example, while an institution operating with basic literacy may create and disseminate a monthly report of all available balances for its restricted funds, an intermediate-level institution can generate a live report that provides employees throughout the museum with status of their funds. The availability of on-demand reporting allows the museum to gradually increase expectations for each program to take more ownership of their financial monitoring. In turn, sharing this information with the development office facilitates external reporting to donors on how their funds are being used.

Advanced Level

Basic literacy institutions are focused on navigating the present. Intermediate literacy institutions are leveraging more modernized processes and tools to discern the present and learn from the past. At peak financial literacy, institutions are able to engage in planning and risk mitigation exercises that prepare them for the future.

An institution seeking to develop advanced financial literacy is more fully realizing the building blocks of the Integration pillar to move toward its goals as a cohesive enterprise. Annual budgeting is aligned with the strategic plan, and financial decisions are made through transparent and accountable structures. Efforts to advance financial practices are guided by change management to ensure their successful implementation across the institution.

Returning to our example of the intermediate-level museum, imagine that the institution advances by building on the uses for the data now available through automated reporting tools. The governance body responsible for implementing the strategic plan may review financial reporting to better understand how the annual budget is supporting the museum's strategic goals. Perhaps governance finds that too much funding is being spent on low-priority projects, and it initiates an effort to revise the budget. Better still, the governance body notes this discrepancy before the budget is approved and makes changes to bring the planned spending into alignment with the strategic plan. Multiple parts of the institution are collaborating and bringing their unique perspectives to analyze, interpret, and act on financial information.

The integrated museum is now focused on enhancing its resilience to future uncertainty. The institution begins to think about long-term resource needs and resource availability by building a multi-year budget and projecting future cash flow. The museum assesses its internal and external risks and takes steps to monitor and manage the greatest risks. A governance body monitors the institution's financial forecast and makes decisions about how to address potential downturns and upswings. The museum is now leveraging the joint capability of all eight FIRM building blocks.

GROWING FINANCIAL LITERACY

Financial literacy cannot be advanced overnight. The FIRM framework helps museums steadily advance through levels of institutional financial literacy until the pillars of Integration and Resilience are fully realized. The building blocks of each pillar are arranged to account for the increasing level of financial literacy needed to successfully implement them. They must be gradually built from the bottom up, building connections between the building blocks along the way.

Institutional and individual financial literacy must be grown in tandem to ensure new capabilities are successfully implemented. As processes and tools are advanced, additional effort needs to be devoted to ensuring that the individual financial literacy of employees is keeping pace.

There are many ways institutions can support employees in growing their financial literacy as institutional advancements are made. As with any change, a key inhibitor to increasing financial literacy is employees' failure to adopt the very procedures designed to help them. It is essential that new financial language, processes, and tools be thoughtfully designed, user-friendly, and accompanied by robust training and support. Sustained engagement and information sharing ensures that employees understand how to incorporate these new capabilities into their work and adapts museum culture to embrace new opportunities to leverage financial information.

FIRM helps museum leaders tackle institutional and individual financial literacy challenges using four techniques: documentation, standardization, simplification, and modernization. Each technique can be used individually or jointly to target the specific financial literacy challenges being addressed.

Documentation

Documentation involves memorializing the actions and processes that museum staff currently carry out. Museum staff are keenly aware of the importance of documentation in the context

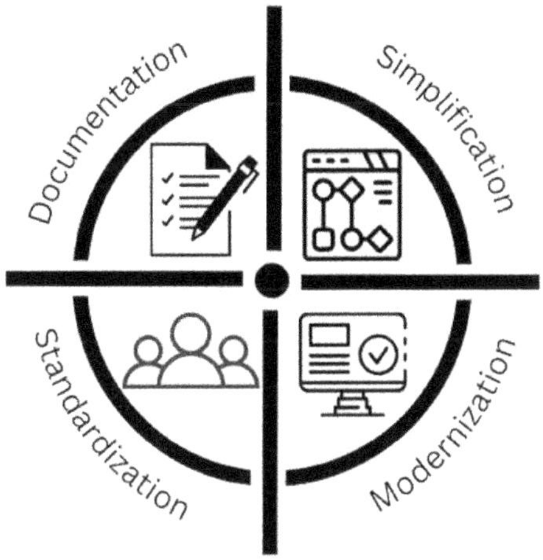

Figure 2.2 Financial Literacy Techniques. *Source*: Ashley Amos.

of the museum's collection or areas of scholarship. The process of recording, cataloging, and managing such information can require a coordinated effort across multiple stakeholders within the museum. By maintaining detailed records, museums ensure their knowledge is maintained for the benefit of future generations.

This same discipline should be applied to financial management. Documenting the museum's financial management roles, responsibilities, and processes ensures continuity. Current employees may have well-established ways of carrying out their financial responsibilities, but the museum must be prepared for when current employees inevitably depart or retire. New employees who take their place need to be equipped with clear, written documentation from day one. Museums risk significant loss of institutional knowledge when they lack the documentation to facilitate this knowledge transfer.

Documentation should begin with gathering all existing guidance and communications. Policy documents and their associated operating procedures should be cataloged and placed in an easily accessible format and location. Informal guidance may have been communicated over time in emails, training sessions, and other materials. Individual employees or supervisors may have created desk guides during employee transitions.

In some cases, simply collecting existing materials and compiling them into formal documentation may be sufficient. In others, the documentation will reveal that existing ways of doing business should be changed. Establishing a documentation baseline is critical to ensuring that a museum does not change its processes without fully understanding how processes are currently operating. In this way, documentation can prove a valuable fact-finding tool in the change management effort related to the three other techniques of standardization, simplification, and modernization.

Standardization

Standardization brings uniformity to financial management procedures, practices, and guidelines. Standardization is needed when multiple ways of doing business have developed over time for the same task. Inconsistent business processes and confusion over how work is accomplished will always limit financial literacy. Processing an invoice or writing a contract may seem like small matters for a museum that should not require much consideration or oversight. But when small matters are not accomplished in a standardized manner, confusion sets in. Valuable time and resources that could be allocated to other matters is lost chasing paper. When staff are on the same page regarding how these tasks are executed, it enhances teamwork and promotes a unified approach to achieving the museum's goals.

Any effort to apply standardization to existing financial practices must necessarily take into account how those practices became inconsistent in the first place. Inconsistencies may be the result of a lack of oversight or clear guidance from the finance office that led to each office coming up with their own approach. Perhaps strong personalities demanded exceptions to standard ways of doing business. Staff may have historically lacked the financial skills to carry out existing policies and procedures, and lack of leadership attention has enabled irregularities to persist. Understanding why and to what extent practices have deviated will enable a museum to select a new standard approach. Following the tenets of change management, standardization should seek minimal disruption to current approaches while meeting the desired end of consistency.

Simplification

Simplification involves streamlining steps to make processes more efficient. Overly complex processes are a barrier to financial literacy. A process that has too many steps, reviews, and approvals may be confusing and time-consuming to navigate. Employees may shy away from engaging with a process when they don't understand what must be done to successfully run the gauntlet of approvals. Those assigned roles in an overly complex process may lose sight of the specific lens they are meant to be applying to their review and contribute to overlaps and gaps with other reviewers.

Worst of all, requests entered into complex processes tend to get stuck somewhere along the workflow with the requestor unable to clearly identify where the request stalled. Unmet needs are a significant reputational risk to the finance office and to the entire museum if the request was in support of an audience- or donor-facing activity. Frustration with complex processes increases the likelihood that staff will begin working outside the established workflow, which contributes to a lack of standardization.

Simplification provides museum staff with clear and concise instructions, enhancing their productivity and reducing administrative burden. By identifying and eliminating inefficiencies, museums can better manage their financial and personnel resources. Streamlined communication channels among staff members foster collaboration across offices and improve understanding of how these processes can be leveraged to carry out their work. Most importantly, simplified financial operations enable museums to respond more quickly to urgent needs or external changes.

Modernization

Modernization involves applying technological solutions to advance financial literacy. Even museums who have effectively documented, standardized, and simplified their financial processes will stagnate without modernization. Financial literacy relies on the perpetual advancement of a museum's capabilities. Without efforts to modernize, a museum cannot fully realize the building blocks of FIRM.

Modernization can enable employees to interact seamlessly, carry out work faster, and track processes more effectively. Requests that were once made via email are now routed through a shared platform. Financial activity once calculated in spreadsheets is now available in an automated report. Outdated software is replaced with a new system with features that align with financial best practices. Each of these examples presents opportunities to advance financial literacy and prevent the institution from lagging behind.

Because modernization involves technology, use of this financial literacy technique requires more significant change management to ensure employees understand the more advanced financial literacy required. Too often, museums simply layer new financial tools over current practices in the hope that modernization will solve ongoing problems. However, without having first steadily advanced financial literacy through standardization, simplification, and documentation, a museum will not be prepared to take the financial literacy leap required by modernization.

Modernization will likely require renewed application of the three other financial literacy techniques to align processes with the new technology. Perhaps existing documentation needs to be updated to demonstrate system navigation to users. The system may provide new opportunities for simplification that were not possible before. On the other hand, modernization may have unexpected negative impacts on standardization efforts. Perhaps a new financial tool enables the creation of multiple workflow pathways based on the office initiating the request. While such complexity may be possible with advanced tools, leaders should consider how this use of this feature runs counter to the goal of improving financial literacy. The chapter on financial tools includes more discussion on how museums can consider the best solution to meet their modernization goals.

Forthcoming chapters will frequently refer back to financial literacy's foundational role in FIRM. Financial literacy collaborates closely with the building blocks of change management, which helps to steady progress, and governance, which provides stable leadership to processes. One or more of the financial literacy techniques should be applied to optimize existing practices, such as budgeting and strategic planning, and support new practices, such as scenario planning or multi-year budgeting, from the ground up.

Part III

THE INTEGRATION PILLAR

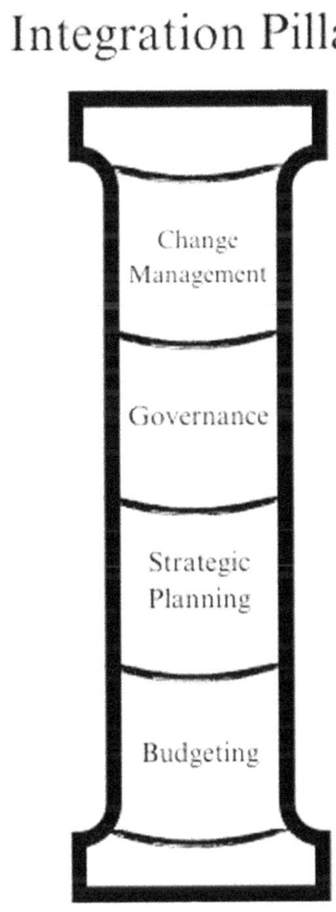

Chapter 3

Budgeting

INTEGRATION BUILDING BLOCK 1

The first building block of the Integration pillar involves the budgeting process. All museums prepare annual budgets. Budgeting is the primary means through which a museum puts its resources into action. Its placement as the first building block recognizes that all further advancements must be built upon a solid budgeting process. This chapter outlines the key components of a robust budgeting process that enable a museum to not just succeed in its annual budgeting but to integrate all other aspects of FIRM into its financial management practices.

Each museum's approach to budgeting has developed based on many factors. Budgets may be driven by the external requirements of public partners, the museum board, or donor reporting and by internal goals of accountability, prioritization, or planning. Depending on the robustness of an institution's budget process, it can require significant time and resources from staff at all levels.

The prioritization required for budgeting can make it one of the few occasions when an institution must work together for a shared purpose. However, because budgeting involves difficult decisions and numerous variables, there is a risk that this annual process gets relegated from a valuable planning tool to a perfunctory exercise.

The annual budgeting process is an opportunity to promote both institutional and individual financial literacy. It is important to establish a shared understanding among participants regarding how the budget is prepared. The annual budgeting process can also enable an institution to reset its financial literacy level through incremental improvements to both budget preparation activities and decision-making.

BUDGET FORMULATION

Before preparing, or formulating, a budget, museum leadership must establish the type of budget being prepared. Providing budgeting participants with clear information about the type of budget being formulated sets the initial boundaries and expectations of the process. For example, a museum that uses cash budgeting would communicate to staff that only the funds currently in hand are available for budgeting; there are no additional resources to meet their needs. Alternatively, a zero-based budget communicates that each budget item must be newly justified and approved for the upcoming year, even if it is a continuing activity.

The process of budget formulation includes the same key elements regardless of the institution. The finance office provides budget instructions and templates and task offices with articulating their needs for the upcoming year. The needs often outpace the resources available, and tough decisions must be made at multiple levels, including by individual offices, the finance office, and museum leadership.

Budgeting can be a frustrating process. No matter the size of the museum, the scope of the exhibit, or importance of the program, budgeting for any project or initiative starts with the question of what are the needs, or uses, that the budget must support. Program and project planning can seem daunting when spending in next year's budget is dependent on hitting this year's milestones. New work may not be able to start until personnel are hired or a contract is in place.

For a museum that operates on a January to December budget year, staff may be asked to begin preparing a budget a year in advance. This means that an expense planned for next December may need to be quantified nearly two years early. Moreover, the budget may require a level of detail for future expenses that can make cost projection feel like guesswork.

A common budgeting pitfall is only thinking about annually recurring expenses. If this year's budget is the starting point for the next budget, new or non-annual costs may be forgotten. Perhaps a piece of IT equipment needs to be replaced every seven years. Perhaps the completion of a capital construction project will create new operations and maintenance costs in future years. Failure to account for these budget changes will result in deferred action, such as letting the IT equipment exceed its scheduled lifespan, or will require tapping into cash reserves to fund the omitted items, such as paying the utility bills for the new facility.

Inversely, a project that was generating annual costs may be coming to a close, and those budget items will not need to recur in the next budget. Continuing those costs out of habit or hedging that the project may be delayed into the next budget year will tie up funds that could support other budget needs.

An additional pain point in budgeting is estimating how much funding, or sources, will be available to support planned spending. Institutions with strong endowment payouts or who have existing cash reserves will have an easier time resourcing their budget needs than those who are relying on the future achievement of fundraising goals. No one has a crystal ball to know how much funding will be raised in the coming year. Even if raised, the funds may be restricted to a specific purpose, only supporting one program or project when many others are in need of resources. Additionally, restricted gifts often include the assumption that a portion of the gift can be used to cover administrative or overhead costs associated with management of the funds. During budgeting, it is important to account for these indirect costs when budgeting for both programmatic and support functions that will use the restricted fund as a source.

After each office completes the estimation of their future needs, the finance office has the difficult task of creating a balanced budget. A balanced budget requires that the uses of funding do not exceed the available sources. This process requires decisions at the highest levels of museum leadership about what programs and projects get funded and what funding requests must be denied. Budget formulation will benefit from leveraging the lessons of the governance building block of FIRM. Governance will help identify the appropriate decision-makers and decision structures to drive budget discussions toward a shared purpose.

When balancing a budget that relies on projected revenue, it can be tempting to continually increase the sources part of the equation to match an ever-growing list of uses. Museum leadership may be eager to support expansion and change initiatives before sufficient funding is in place.

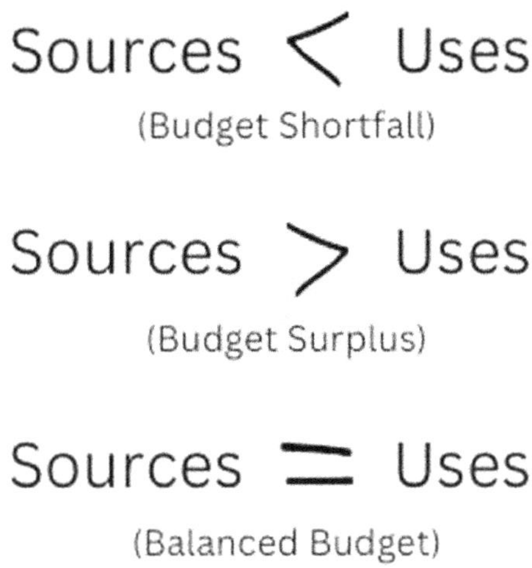

Figure 3.1 Balancing Sources and Uses. *Source*: Ashley Amos.

Over several years, the Museum of Contemporary Art in Los Angeles gradually drained its cash reserves and borrowed from restricted funds to cover its operating costs.[1] Despite declining resources, the museum increased staffing by 25 percent and invested in additional educational programs and a curatorial department.[2] The museum struggled to remain open in the midst of fiscal crisis and faced public scrutiny including damaging media reporting and an inquiry from the California attorney general that did not result in charges.[3] The museum was able to recover in the short term by cutting the budget nearly 30 percent and securing donations to cover operating costs while it engaged in a longer-term campaign to grow its endowment.[4]

It is critical that budgeting comes with a clear set of assumptions that can help address some of the unknowns. This is where active leadership from the finance office is critical. The finance office can provide all manner of assumptions such as anticipated employee pay increases and guidance on estimating contract costs. The finance office can also help offices break down what can seem like a massive undertaking into more digestible bites. For example, budget formulation guidance could state that existing personnel should be budgeted before the purchase of goods and services is considered. Taking a programmatic view, guidance could state that ongoing projects need to be budgeted to completion before new work is contemplated. These assumptions can help ensure all offices are thinking about budgeting in the same way and lead to a more informed result.

BUILDING A BUDGET CYCLE

Even with a strong set of assumptions to guide budget formulation, the most important message a finance office can reinforce during budgeting is that a budget is just a plan. Plans can and will change with new information that challenges the original assumptions. Too often, an institution will do the work to formulate an annual budget, deliver it to the board, and declare success. The budget has served its purpose, but as soon as it is finalized (or maybe even before that) its assumptions have been overcome by events. The landscape has

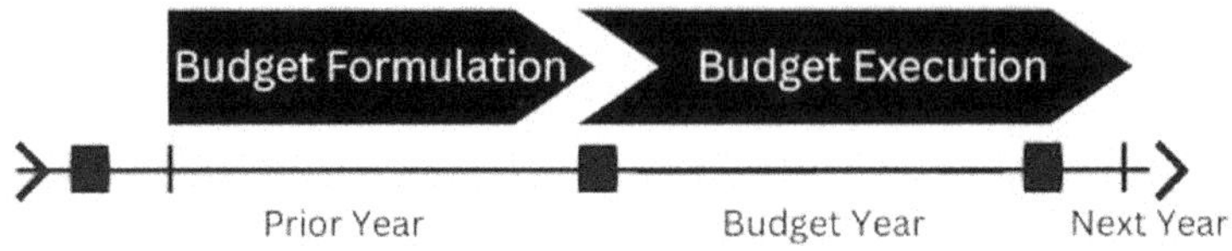

Figure 3.2 Annual Budgeting Timeline. *Source*: Ashley Amos.

changed, and the budget may not even be worth the paper it is printed on. The institution then navigates the coming year as a series of curve balls that little can be done to prepare for.

A significant amount of time and resources are lost when financial planning ends with the adoption of an annual budget. If a budget is viewed as a plan, then the plan can change. The plan can be updated when assumptions no longer match reality. A budget must be treated as a living document, with a standardized schedule that begins with formulation and continues throughout the budget year as the museum monitors how its budget is being carried out or executed. This schedule is referred to as a budget cycle.

The budget cycle helps institutions understand changing conditions that necessitate revisions to the original budget. Budget revisions should occur on a regular tempo throughout the budget cycle—at least quarterly or monthly depending on the institution's level of financial literacy and the dynamic nature of its budget environment. As a museum sets up its budget cycle, it is important to document the timeline for budget formulation and regular budget revisions during budget execution. Employees should be trained on the timeline with refresher training each year to ensure individual financial literacy is sustained.

It may seem odd that the phrase budget cycle implies a circular shape, yet the timeline is linear. Each budget year will have its own linear timeline from the start of formulation to the year's close, but the cyclical nature of budgeting begins to be understood when multiple years of budgeting are considered together. It is common for formulation for next year to be carried out while this year's budget is still in the midst of execution. In an institution with lower financial literacy in budgeting, these two budget cycles may be carried out independently. For example, a museum may use the current year's formulated budget as the starting

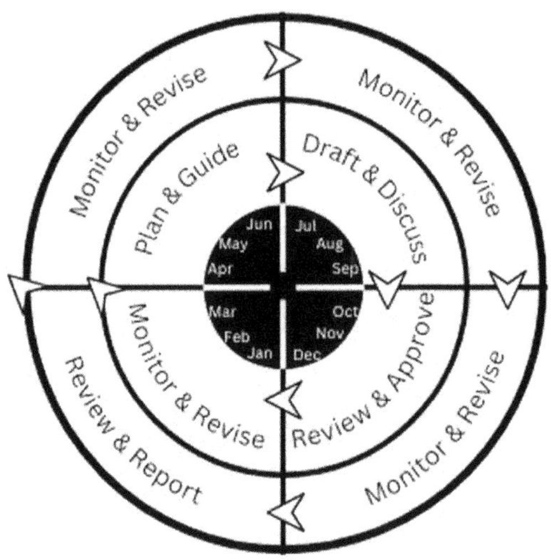

Figure 3.3 Annual Budgeting Cycle. *Source*: Ashley Amos.

point for the next budget, even though they are now several months into budget execution and plans have changed.

As an institution advances, it can begin applying the new financial information gleaned from execution of the current year budget thus far to help formulate next year's budget. This feedback loop can help museums make their budgets more realistic to the progress they are making in various projects and programs (uses) and have more accurate estimations of the resources that will be available by the start of the next year (sources). A budget that leverages this financial information will be better positioned to balance sources and uses.

BUDGET EXECUTION

Budget execution is the phase of the budget cycle when the budget is carried out. The plan has been made, the budget year has begun, and the museum is beginning to pay staff, purchase goods and services, and receive revenue. To ensure that revenue and spending don't diverge from the budget over time, it is important to monitor execution against the budget.

At a basic level of financial literacy, budget execution monitoring may be carried out periodically, such as the end of each month or quarter, through manual calculations. An institution with more advanced literacy will leverage financial tools that produce reports based on data in its financial systems. Regardless of method, the calculation is the same. Spending to-date is subtracted from the total budget to understand how much remains available for spending during the remainder of the budget year.

To ensure an accurate view of the remaining budget, the calculation of spending must include both those funds that have been paid out for goods or services (expenses) and those that have been set aside for anticipated payments (obligations and commitments). Failing to include the funds that have been set aside as commitments and obligations in the spending calculation risks that the museum accidentally promises the same funds to more than one use.

For example, a museum may budget $100,000 for translation services with a plan to contract with a vendor at the start of the budget year. Before announcing the need to potential bidders, the museum should set aside—or commit—the $100,000 budgeted amount to ensure it is available when a vendor is selected. When the contract is awarded, the $100,000 commitment will become an obligation in the amount of the successful vendor's bid, say $98,000. The commitment of the remaining $2,000 may now be removed as it is not needed to cover the actual value of the contract. This $2,000 is now free to be applied to another budget need.

Over the coming months, the vendor will render its translation services and regularly invoice the museum for the costs. Each time the museum pays an invoice, a portion of the obligation is recorded as an expense. If the first invoice is for $1,000, the museum will now show $1,000 in expenses and $97,000 in remaining obligation on the contract. The obligation will continue to decrease until the total value of the contract is expensed or the work of the contract is otherwise complete.

If the museum in this example was calculating its remaining budget, it should subtract the total amount of commitments, obligations, and expenses related to this contract from its budget. Inclusion of only the first invoice payment of $1,000 would vastly understate the $98,000 contract it has entered into with the translation services vendor.

Table 3.1 Tracking Planned Contract Costs from Budget to Expense

Action	*Budget*	*Commitment*	*Obligation*	*Expense*
Translation services added in budget formulation	$100,000			
Competition of translation services contract		$100,000		
Contract award to winning vendor	−$2,000	−$100,000	$98,000	
First vendor invoice			$97,000	$1,000

Source: Ashley Amos.

LIVING WITH DYNAMIC NUMBERS

Over the course of a fiscal year, budget execution monitoring will generate a significant amount of financial data. The dynamic nature of financial data can be confusing to those who struggle with financial literacy. Budget execution data can diverge from the original budget assumptions for two primary reasons: an increase or decrease in revenue expectations (sources) and an uptick or slowdown in spending (uses). More analysis of the data is needed to understand what variables are driving this change—does it relate to how the museum is hiring employees or issuing contracts, the natural cadence of fundraising activities, changes in visitation, or economic conditions?

The finance office plays an important role in working with museum leadership and each office to analyze financial data and help them make decisions based on what is learned. Using the budget cycle to establish a regular cadence for budget monitoring and revision will create opportunities for this support to be provided in an organized manner with consistent reinforcement of financial literacy.

A museum with comprehensive financial tools will increase the financial literacy needed to manage the dynamic nature of financial data. Financial tools provide a means to systematically capture data and present the same view each time the tools are consulted. For example, if an office is building its own spreadsheet to track its budget, there is the potential that human error or changes to the calculation method will create discrepancies in the data. Attempts to compare multiple iterations of this manual calculation may result in confusion about why the numbers have changed and lead to distrust of the data. A report that draws directly from the financial system will significantly increase confidence in the data.

Even with financial tools in place, the finance office must ensure museum staff have the individual financial literacy needed to analyze the reports. Analysis requires isolating those variables that have changed the financial data over the period of time being reviewed and making decisions about whether and how to change course.

The first budget execution variable relates to unanticipated changes in sources. If a private donor provides an unexpected gift that is restricted to one purpose, the finance office can work with the relevant office to spend those funds rather than the source that was originally budgeted. Alternatively, perhaps a donor has not yet provided funds that were previously pledged to the museum and relied on in the budget. The finance office must review the ups and downs of various sources throughout budget execution to make decisions about how to rebalance the budget. The use of unanticipated restricted funds for a project will allow the funds that were originally budgeted to be reapplied to other museum needs, such as areas where fundraising was lower than anticipated, or may be held by the finance office as resources for the next budget year.

The second budget execution variable relates to uses: whether the planned spending envisioned by the original budget is occurring as expected. Perhaps the calculation of the remaining budget for a program shows that spending is projected to outpace budgeted resources. Alternatively, perhaps spending is unexpectedly low because a budgeted project has not yet started. An external event may prompt the need for an activity that was not in the original budget. In all cases, finance can work with the office and museum leadership during budget execution to make decisions about how the budget should be revised to address these realities. For example, the resources that were previously provided for the delayed project could be reassigned to the emergent activity or the program experiencing cost overruns.

Budget execution monitoring not only enables an institution to adapt to change but is a valuable source of data about organizational behavior. If a museum conducts a quarterly budget review, it will have four versions of a revised budget in addition to the original. All five versions can be viewed as a data set to show trends across the institution. Are there certain seasons of heavier spending? Were initial budget estimates too low or too high? Did some offices make more budget changes than others? Identifying these patterns can help the finance office better understand the museum's operations, leading to improved budget assumptions and more consistent budget performance in future years. This is the budget cycle at work.

BUILDING A BUDGET PLAYBOOK

As an institution advances the sophistication of its budget cycle, it is essential to ensure individual financial literacy is promoted in tandem. The budget cycle for any one budget year can last nearly two years—or even longer if a museum begins its formulation process early. Each time an employee is asked to begin formulating a budget, it will have been a year since the last time that task was performed. Or worse, the experienced employee has since departed and a new employee who has never participated in formulation is in their place. Museums can lose significant ground when they lack the institutional memory to effectively repeat—let alone improve upon—their budget cycle each year.

Documentation such as procedures, desk guides, and workflows enable the individual financial literacy needed for employees to complete discrete tasks within the budget cycle. However, it is important that the detailed nature of these documents does not leave employees unsure of how their actions fit into the larger budget cycle. A budget playbook can be a valuable high-level guide to the who, what, when, and why of the budget cycle.

The key component of a budget playbook is the budget cycle calendar, which provides the "when" for museum staff. Presentation of the entire lifecycle of a budget will help ground employees in how to plan their time and allows them to look beyond the next deadline. The timeline also sets expectations for the key decision points throughout the budget cycle so employees will understand that funding requests may be approved, denied, or changed as decisions are reached. This information helps answer the "why" that can otherwise lead to distrust of the process if employees don't understand the reason a request failed to move forward.

The playbook also lists the key roles involved in the budget cycle at the museum. This will provide museum staff with the "who" of the budget cycle. Roles and responsibilities can get blurred over time if accountability is not documented and reinforced. The playbook will not be a comprehensive listing of every position in the museum that spends some amount of time working on the budget, but rather a description of key role types that can be assigned.

Table 3.2 Answering Questions through a Budget Playbook

Questions answered through a budget playbook	
Who	Define roles and responsibilities for participants in the budget process
What	Provide access to training, templates, and terminology
When	Create a timeline of key dates in the budget cycle
Why	Define decision points in the budget cycle that may result in approval or denial of requests

For example, a budget drafter role is the individual designated by their office to physically enter the budget items into the designated template. The budget drafter may be a member of administrative or operations staff or a project manager. The budget drafter role differs from a budget approver, who may be the operations manager or head of an office. The budget approver is responsible for reviewing the budget after it is drafted and making decisions before elevating it to the next level.

Museums may have many roles to name and define based on the number of layers of review and approval they apply at various stages of the budget cycle. These roles are not likely to align with an employee's formal job title, so it is important to ensure individual employees know they have been designated to take on these responsibilities and adequately trained to carry them out.

The budget playbook should include a glossary of any budgetary and financial terms used throughout the document or that employees will encounter when entering their budgets into the designated templates. Examples of the templates or links to where they are located can be included. The playbook can also provide links to existing training materials for employees who are new to the process or need to refresh their skills. Together, these tools provide a consolidated guide to "how" employees will carry out the budget cycle.

The playbook should be updated and reevaluated on an annual basis. Institutions and employees change over time, and this maintenance effort will ensure the playbook reflects any advancements in the budget process, changes to budget cycle timelines, or updates to training materials.

Implementing a budget cycle is a whole-of-institution effort. Using the budget playbook to define roles, terminology, and timelines is an important part of developing a shared financial language and shared understanding of how everyone contributes to the larger process. The playbook is a critical step toward institutional integration as an opportunity to break down silos and reinforce the notion of a shared financial ecosystem.

THE BUDGET AS A PERFORMANCE DOCUMENT

As an institution advances its budgeting capability to higher levels of financial literacy, financial data may be augmented with performance data. The development and tracking of performance measures can help internal and external stakeholders get a better understanding of how spending is supporting the museum's overall mission.

The incorporation of performance measures into budget documents became standard practice for federal departments and agencies with the passage of the Government Performance and Results Act (GPRA) in 1993.[5] This legislation set standards for an annual performance report that must be submitted with annual budget requests. Each year, museums that receive direct federal funding must submit to Congress a report on performance measures and make it publicly available.[6]

Whether a museum is subject to a similar external requirement or measuring its own performance, it is important to determine what kinds of performance a museum wants to measure and communicate to its stakeholders. At their core, performance measures are tracking progress toward the museum's goals.

Performance measures can be presented both qualitatively and quantitatively. Qualitative measures are descriptive and often subjective in nature. They involve qualities or characteristics that cannot be easily measured or expressed numerically. This can include quotes from visitors that provide insight into their experience at the museum. Qualitative information can have varying levels of complexity, such as comparing a visitor's perspectives on an exhibit before and after experiencing it. The accomplishments and milestones of projects and initiatives can also provide qualitative insights into how the museum is progressing toward its strategic goals. The design of a new exhibit, the acquisition of an important collection, and the completion of a new data privacy plan are all examples of qualitative performance.

Quantitative performance measures are data or information that can be expressed using numbers. The availability of quantitative data will vary depending on the level of institutional financial literacy. Most museums will track data about public access, such as the number of days open to the public, annual visitors, and special events hosted. A museum will organically have other information related to certain projects and initiatives that are quantifiable and can begin collecting and tracking data to demonstrate progress toward these efforts. For example, efforts to digitize or grow the collection can be quantified by tracking the number of photographs digitized or works added to the collection.

As the museum's level of financial literacy continues to increase, it may create more advanced quantitative data by integrating performance measures with financial data. The number of photographs that were digitized in a year can be divided by the total budget of the digitization project to present an average digitization cost per photograph.

Performance measures will change over time as ongoing work is completed and new work begins. However, as long as work is ongoing, a museum should plan to report the same performance measures in each budget tied to the prior year's performance. A consistent approach enables stakeholders to understand the trajectory of multi-year work.

The most valuable aspect of including prior year performance metrics in the budget document is to remind stakeholders that the dollars spent by the museum have measurable, tangible outcomes. They can take pride in the role they play in contributing to and supporting that work.

As discussed in the context of budget execution, the budget document is a significant undertaking and should not be set aside after it is prepared. The value of the budget only increases as museums with advancing financial literacy add components of qualitative and quantitative performance measures. The benefits may be felt outside the budget realm as well.

The significant intellectual capital that has been invested in the collection and integration of financial and performance-based information can serve multiple other museum purposes. Information assembled for the budget can serve as a resource for internal communications about the progress on the strategic plan, external outreach materials, and fundraising proposals to potential donors. The finance office can collaborate with museum offices to summarize financial data and present select performance measures to stakeholders based on their interests or concerns.

FIRM CONNECTIONS

Budgeting is the first building block of the Integration pillar because nearly every institution will begin the FIRM journey with some version of a budget process in place. Building on the foundation of existing financial literacy, budgeting provides regular opportunities to foster other integration principles of governance and change management and to operationalize strategic planning. As we will explore later in this book, a robust budgeting process becomes a vehicle for incorporating risk management, scenario planning, multi-year budgeting, and financial tools to support the Resilience pillar of FIRM.

Chapter 4

Strategic Planning

INTEGRATION BUILDING BLOCK 2

Strategic planning is the next building block of FIRM's Integration pillar. A strategic plan is an essential tool for integration because it holistically expresses the purpose and direction of an institution. Strategic plans are routinely developed throughout the corporate and nonprofit community. However, many institutions struggle to translate long-term strategic goals into actions. Strategic planning cannot succeed without a direct connection to the annual budgeting process. Because the office responsible for strategic planning is unlikely to be the finance office, the integration of these processes requires a whole-of-institution effort in which budget owners are armed with the tools to channel ambitious goals into targeted allocation of available resources.

This chapter discusses how to develop a strategic plan, which may be well known to museum leaders that already engage in a strategic planning process. The components of a strategic plan are reviewed with an emphasis on clear definitions that set up future implementation for success. A well-crafted strategic plan effectively flows from broad statements down to defined actions and measurable progress. Such actions and process can only be achieved through an enduring tether to the budgeting process. Anything else is simply a piece of paper that will fall short of becoming the lodestar the museum seeks.

Before venturing deeper into this topic, it is important to clarify the distinction between a *strategic plan* and *strategic planning*. A strategic plan is a static document that endures for multiple years. This comprehensive document outlines an organization's long-term goals and the actions needed to achieve them. It sets institutional direction through a statement of mission and vision, analysis of current and upcoming opportunities and challenges, and establishment of goals and objectives that define the institution's aspirations.

The development of a strategic plan is just one step of the broader strategic planning process that actively charts progress in implementing the strategic plan. Strategic planning as an institutional process involves following through on the goals and objectives through ongoing monitoring.

FIRM CONNECTION: GOVERNANCE

Strategic planning is part of the Integration pillar of FIRM because an institution working together to carry out a shared strategic plan will necessarily be more integrated than an unguided institution. But before a strategic plan can contribute to integration, it needs to be drafted with the help of another Integration building block: governance. Governance is critical at the start of strategic plan development to define participants and their roles and responsibilities in the process. The continuation of this governance will also be essential to the transition from drafting to carrying out the strategic plan, as we will discuss later in this chapter.

During the development of a strategic plan, governance should include the museum leaders who will make decisions about what will be included in the plan as it begins to take shape. Governance helps guide the process and ensures the resulting document reflects an institution-wide view. The promulgation of a new strategic plan will likely need to undergo approval by the museum's board. As such, involvement of the board should be considered in the design of strategic planning governance.

Below governance is a larger structure of participants in the strategic plan development. Representatives from across museum programs and offices provide insights based on their areas of expertise to support strategic goal setting.

The most important role in strategic plan development is a facilitator who can help keep discussions on track and design exercises and activities to stimulate thinking. A museum that has an office responsible for strategic planning may have an in-house facilitator or the museum can hire an external consultant. The facilitator can help participants think about the institution from multiple viewpoints—including museum leaders, stakeholders, the public, and employees—because each will be part of the future picture they are assembling. The facilitator will also find opportunities to gain insights and feedback from representatives of these different viewpoints if they have not already been identified as participants in strategic plan development.

DEVELOPING A STRATEGIC PLAN

Strategic planning is intended to focus on where the institution wants to go, but it is impossible to ignore where the institution is starting from. A museum that views much of its mission areas as interrelated may find strategic planning to be a difficult undertaking. A siloed organization may have the opposite problem: work areas may be so segmented that it is difficult to develop a cohesive strategic plan that encompasses all of them.

A common misstep is to conflate "what do we do now?" with "what is our desired future state?" There is a risk, especially if the work of an institution has developed without the guidance of a strategic plan, that the process of strategic planning will be used to validate existing areas of work by forcing a future state that makes room for all of them. A truly open vision of the future requires acknowledgment that some current work may not be a long-term fit. Likewise, new areas of work may be needed to help an institution achieve its strategic plan.

Because a strategic plan is a document developed at a moment in time, an important early step is to determine the intended time horizon of the plan. The duration of the strategic plan impacts more than how long an institution expects to wait before taking up the planning process again. The word strategic necessarily implies that the plan sets the institution's trajectory for the mid- to long-term. A strategic plan with a 1–2-year lifespan would barely outlast a single budget cycle and would not add much value as a strategic tool.

An institution may choose to link the strategic plan to the duration of its director's employment contract. This would ensure that museum leadership and the strategic plan are always aligned. A newly hired museum director would have the opportunity to develop and implement their own strategic plan, rather than being beholden to the previous director's plan.

The timeline of the strategic plan also determines what goal setting looks like. A strategic plan that charts the path for the next ten years is going to have much more ambitious aims than a plan with a five-year duration. The aims envisioned by the strategic plan should be achievable within the timeframe allotted. Strategic plans that are too ambitious will set the institution up for failure rather than success and may be abandoned as irrelevant or unfeasible.

Brainstorming

A SWOT diagram is one of many brainstorming exercises that can stimulate thinking for strategic planning.[1] SWOT refers to the strengths, weaknesses, opportunities, and threats that an institution faces both internally and externally.[2] A facilitator can lead participants in an analysis of each of these four elements.

Too small or homogenous of a participant group may limit the value of a SWOT if participants' knowledge of the museum is largely the same. Another potential limitation is participants only thinking about the strengths, weaknesses, opportunities, and threats of the current environment. The strategic plan will be a future-oriented document, so the SWOT must also look ahead. The facilitator can help expand the SWOT's scope by encouraging thinking about how the museum would fare in future scenarios.

Participants can draw upon resources such as financial statements, surveys, trends at similar institutions, and stakeholder feedback to contribute additional perspectives to the brainstorming effort. For example, financial performance data would provide context to the museum's ability to grow and sustain itself. Visitor trends may be indicative of specific market advantages.

An institution that carries out the building blocks of the Resilience pillar will have many more resources on which to draw for its conception of its future state. Risk management, scenario planning, multi-year budgeting, and use of financial tools will all contribute additional data points and views of the future.

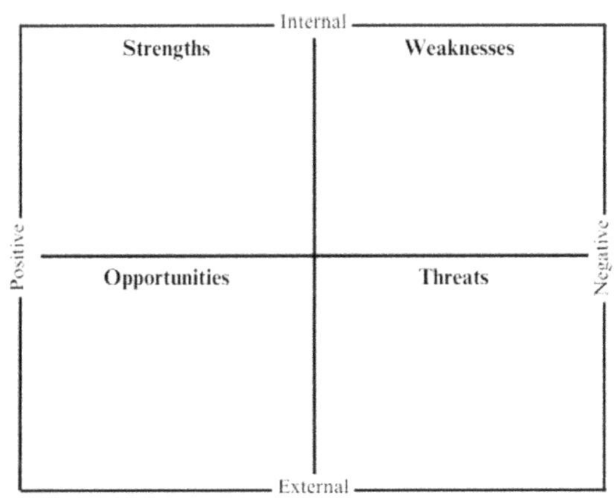

Figure 4.1 SWOT Analysis. *Source*: Ashley Amos.

Strengths are those areas where an institution has an advantage. Throughout this chapter we will consider the example of a folk art museum embarking on the development of a strategic plan. Perhaps the participants in this museum's SWOT exercise identify this list of strengths: the museum's exclusive collection by a well-known artist, proximity to public transportation in a budding tourism district, affordability of admission fees when compared to other nearby museums, and availability of art acquisition funds that will allow the museum to add new material to its collection.

Weaknesses are the inverse of strengths. Weaknesses are those areas where an institution performs poorly or where improvement is necessary for growth. For our folk art museum, weaknesses may include a deteriorating facility, a minimal online presence, and exhibits that lack interactive experiences.

Opportunities are those areas that could positively impact the institution's performance or create new possibilities for growth. Opportunities are favorable conditions that, if leveraged, could lead to future areas of strength. An example of an opportunity for our folk art museum could be recent interest from the tourism board promoting local museums or the upcoming twenty-fifth anniversary of the museum's opening.

Threats are factors that could pose challenges or risks to the museum's success. Threats can also be areas where the museum's performance may fall behind compared to other similar institutions. Threats can turn into weaknesses if they come to fruition. Examples of threats to our folk art museum are if fundraising fails to keep pace with potential inflation or if a cyberattack causes a breach of sensitive museum information.

Participants should identify as many items in each SWOT category as they can think of. Ideas can be written with markers on a whiteboard or arranged on a wall with sticky notes. The facilitator may have a software tool to help organize suggestions into a digital diagram. The facilitator can then help participants group or summarize similar items that overlap. The SWOT process helps an institution gain a realistic understanding of how it performs in the market and how that performance may change over time. Participants can then leverage the SWOT as a profile of the institution's characteristics to help its strategic plan take shape.

COMPONENTS OF A STRATEGIC PLAN

A strategic plan has four main components: mission, vision, goals, and objectives. This structure begins at the broadest possible view of an institution and gradually narrows to become more specific about its future direction.

The definitions and terms used for these four components can vary, and different facilitators may recommend their own approaches to formulate them. This section provides a general description of the components to establish a shared baseline for discussion of how the strategic plan can be used to drive the strategic planning building block of FIRM.

There are multiple approaches to preparing a strategic plan, which can make the embarking on its development seem overwhelming. A strong facilitator can help a museum understand how different approaches can create a strategic plan that exemplifies an institution's unique character and culture.

Facilitators may also include additional components based on their strategic planning approach and the needs of the institution. However, it should be cautioned that more complex strategic plan structures require clear delineation between concepts. The creation of overlapping components could cause confusion among strategic planning participants, stakeholders, and employees and hamper the success of the strategic plan.

Mission

A mission statement begins with an institution's purpose: why it exists, who it serves, and what distinguishes it from other similar institutions. A mission statement is not a static picture of the museum, so it should not be such a specific description of current activities that it quickly becomes outdated. The mission is the path that the institution will walk as it pursues its vision of the future.

One way to represent this forward motion is to articulate how the museum will go about its work. In pairing together the institution's purpose and approach, the mission statement will feel relevant to both the current and the future state of the museum. The mission should be realistic within the duration of the strategic plan. It will not benefit the institution to set such an aspirational mission that it cannot be realized. Save the aspirations for the vision statement.

If the museum has a board-approved charter or has been established by a legislative act, these should be used as the guidepost for developing a mission statement. Some museums may already have mission and vision statements before embarking on strategic plan development. Because these two components lead and shape the rest of the strategic plan, it is important to start the development process by reviewing existing statements and evaluating whether they continue to represent the direction of the institution.

Mission statement development often starts with disjointed phrases that address one or more aspects of the institution's purpose. Throughout the process, participants can try to string them together in different ways and identify where there are overlaps or gaps. Participants may share drafts of the mission statement with various stakeholders to understand if the resulting language feels like an accurate representation of the institution. This process may repeat through many rounds of feedback. An iterative approach will not only improve the final product but will also contribute to change management efforts by allowing more people to be part of the process.

A mission statement can vary in length from a short phrase to multiple sentences. A museum should avoid getting too wordy as this may signal that it is trying to do too many things. The mission should carve out a unique role for the museum without being confusing or complicated. Conversely, a mission statement should not be so brief that it amounts to an advertising slogan or tagline. This would not tell a visitor, employee, or community member much about what the museum does.

The mission statement for our folk art museum example might read: "Encouraging understanding and appreciation of folk art by collecting and preserving works that illustrate the diverse artistic heritage of our region through dynamic and engaging exhibits." The language chosen is unique to the particular institution, speaking to what the museum specializes in and the community it serves. The language also makes broader assertions about how it wants to go about its work. This language conveys to employees what they are contributing to and speaks to visitors and the wider community about what the museum values.

It is worth noting that the above mission statement incorporates values and principles as part of the institution's description of how it approaches its work. Statements of values or principles speak to the institution's culture: how it wants to carry out its work or how it treats employees and visitors.[3] Some strategic plan approaches will define an institution's core values or guiding principle as a separate component from mission, which will add to the plan's complexity.[4]

Vision

A vision is a concise statement that outlines the organization's view of the future. A vision should be part aspiration and part inspiration. It imagines how the world will be changed for the better if the institution is successful in carrying out its mission.

For an institution that does not have a global reach, it can feel strange to make broad pronouncements about changing the world. It can also feel like a lot of pressure to divine the future without resorting to wild speculation. Another way to think about a vision is simply to ask what the institution is aiming toward. If the mission is the path the institution sets itself on, then the vision is what it hopes to reach at the end of that path.

The vision can be thought of as the institutional equivalent of the common job interview question "where do you see yourself in ten years?" The vision addresses how an institution would know it has succeeded in its mission and whether it has had the desired influence on the world. The facilitator can walk participants through various exercises to stimulate thinking about these questions.

Guidelines about length apply to mission and vision statements alike. If anything, a vision may be even shorter—up to twenty words—to ensure the institution's aspirations are clear and memorable. If participants have come up with multiple vision ideas, consider distilling them into one overarching view of the future rather than stringing the phrases together into a lengthy statement.

Our folk art museum may set a vision of the future where "Creative expression is valued as a means of connecting people to their shared humanity across cultures and traditions." This vision statement is a natural extension of the museum's mission statement, so the employee or stakeholder reading it can understand how carrying out the museum's mission will contribute to this aspirational future.

Mission and vision statements should be drafted in tandem so the resulting language is complementary. The two statements do not necessarily need to be prepared in a particular sequence. Some institutions may find it easiest to define what they do and how they do it before building their vision for the future. Inversely, a museum could start with a vision of what it wants to achieve and then build a mission around how it will get there. There is no wrong way to go about developing these two components of a strategic plan.

Whether an institution starts with its mission or vision, neither should be considered complete until both are complete. It can be difficult to build one component if the other is not a strong counterpart. An institution that continues to get stuck while drafting its vision may realize something is lacking in its mission statement, or vice versa. It may work best to move back and forth between drafts of these statements, as the brainstorming process for one may lead to potential language for the other. Continue iterating and soliciting stakeholder feedback until both statements fully characterize the institution.

Together, the vision and mission are going to be the most visible components of a strategic plan. An institution is likely to display its vision and mission on its website and in printed materials, on public financial documents, and in meetings with employees. These statements help signal to stakeholders and potential donors why they should be involved with the institution. They can inspire employees, fostering a sense of shared purpose and motivation.

Repeating mission and vision statements can only do so much. Incorporating mission and vision into institutional culture requires concerted effort throughout the life of the strategic plan. As we will discuss more during strategic plan implementation, these statements must become the lens through which all potential decisions are viewed.

Goals

Once a mission and vision are established, goals will broadly define what the institution wants to achieve. Goals are statements of what needs to be accomplished to achieve a desired result. Goals are driven by the same institutional purpose that underpins mission, and they are the means through which the museum carries out its mission in pursuit of its vision. A goal that seems disconnected from the mission or vision will not have the desired effect of signaling the museum's direction to employees and stakeholders.

Goals point an institution in the direction of long-term change from the status quo. Approaches vary as to whether goals should be considered achievable within the timeline of the strategic plan or whether they should signify continuous effort. Regardless of the approach, goals should be written in a way that sets clear expectations for the objectives that follow. If a goal is difficult to understand, break down into detailed actions, measure progress toward, or accomplish in a timely manner, the museum may be better off focusing its strategic energy on something else.

Consider our folk art museum example. Perhaps the museum determines it wants to deliver the best visitor experience to as many people as possible. The museum may draft a goal to "Expand and deepen audience engagement." The goal speaks to the broad purpose of audience engagement, which links back similar sentiments in the mission and vision statements. The direction to "expand and deepen" points to two lines of effort that can be broken down into specific actions. Depending on how many actions the museum undertakes to expand its audience and deepen their engagement, it is clear that the museum can continuously pursue this goal through the life of its strategic plan and beyond.

Information gathered and analyzed during the SWOT and other brainstorming exercises help the museum formulate its goals. If the folk art museum has already identified opportunities that would increase its visitorship, then a goal concerning expanding its audience makes sense. However, if one of its weaknesses is that the number of visitors has been steadily declining, then the museum may want to focus this goal solely on deepening engagement with the audience it has, rather than setting an unrealistic expectation for significant growth.

This is just one goal of several that our folk art museum will create for its strategic plan. The number of goals needs to be scaled based on the size of the museum and the scope of its mission and vision. Having only two goals may mean that the museum is not thinking about its strategic plan on a large enough scale or that the museum is combining ideas into compound goals that need to be split up. Nor should the museum have twenty goals. Establishing a goal is setting a strategic priority. A museum of any size will struggle to simultaneously implement a voluminous list of priorities. Offices won't have the resources to carry out numerous goals and employees may feel overburdened by the expectations they create. A strategic plan with four to six goals will be better scaled to make the ambitions achievable.

Objectives

If goals outline what an institution aims to achieve, then objectives break down the actions needed to reach those aims. Objectives outline the steps or actions that contribute to accomplishing the larger goal.

As alluded to in the goals section above, objectives should be specific, measurable, achievable, relevant, and time-bound.[5] Known by the acronym SMART, these five principles help guide an institution to creating objectives that quantify and track the progress needed to achieve the objective.[6] SMART is not an exact recipe; the words themselves have been recast to meet various needs since they were first defined.[7] Some objectives may not be perfectly suited to all five elements. However, keeping SMART in mind as a guide will help ensure objectives are written as effectively as they can be.

Let's look at how our folk art museum example would break down one of its goals into multiple objectives leveraging the SMART guidelines.

Goal 1: Expand and deepen audience engagement

- Objective 1: Increase visitor satisfaction ratings by 15 percent within the next three years
- Objective 2: Increase attendance among underrepresented communities by 25 percent within the next seven years
- Objective 3: Increase student visits by 20 percent over the next five years

Well-crafted and implemented objectives encourage progress without becoming overwhelming. The completion of an objective should provide a sense of accomplishment toward the larger strategic goal, boosting morale and motivation among employees. Individuals and teams can see their contributions and the impact of their efforts, which can increase employee engagement and dedication to the museum's mission and vision.

The development of goals and objectives is another important opportunity to engage employees and other stakeholders who are not active participants in the strategic planning process. Sharing the draft language can help identify the need to create more distinction between goals and objectives. Those who will be responsible for carrying out the objectives can assess how realistic and achievable the goals and objectives are based on their current capabilities and limitations. Early engagement can also jumpstart change management and communication efforts that will occur when the strategic plan is rolled out.

Multiple objectives should be built for each goal. Objectives break down the goal into actions that align with the responsibilities of specific offices or teams. This both sets expectations and creates accountability for managers and employees to contribute to the museum's goals. A goal with multiple objectives that are each assigned to different offices will help them understand how their separate responsibilities contribute to a larger shared effort.

Some goals are interconnected and work on their objectives needs to be synchronized. For example, imagine our folk art museum's second goal relates to enhancing its collection.

Table 4.1 SMART Guidelines

SPECIFIC	What are you trying to accomplish?
MEASURABLE	How will you know you are on track?
ACHIEVABLE	How will you accomplish your objective?
RELEVANT	Does the objective align with your goal?
TIME-BOUND	When will the objective be accomplished?

Source: Ashley Amos.

There may be several areas where new items in the collection could be displayed with interactive elements that also serve the goal to deepen audience experience. Objectives for each goal should consider interdependencies and opportunities for crosscutting progress.

In addition to goals and objectives, some strategic plan approaches will include the development of strategies and tactics. If goals and objectives define what an institution will do, strategies and tactics will define how the institution will do it. Just as a goal can be accomplished through many objectives, a strategy can be broken down into multiple approaches as tactics. Institutions that seek to include these additional components in their strategic plan should ensure their facilitator can help participants, stakeholders, and employees distinguish between the four terms both during development and after rollout.

STRATEGIC PLAN IMPLEMENTATION

The completion of a strategic plan is very time-consuming and is often considered a watershed moment in an institution's growth. Rolling out a strategic plan to employees and other stakeholders is a significant change management effort. An institution may host information sessions, prepare summary documents, and encourage individual offices to discuss their role in the strategic plan.

This can be a time of uncertainty for employees as they wonder how the new strategic plan will change the work that they do. They may question their value if they do not see their work area fully represented in the strategic plan. More jaded employees may write off the strategic plan as one of many they have seen come and go in their careers. An active change management and communication approach throughout the drafting process will help mitigate these concerns by getting more insights and collaboration from employees early on. But once the document is released, it is incumbent on museum leaders to help employees understand what happens next.

An institution should not simply roll out its strategic plan, post it on the website, and then await the next scheduled update five or ten years down the road. The future state envisioned in the strategic plan will only be realized through active engagement throughout its lifespan. The use of implementation plans, monitoring, prioritization, and resource planning will ensure that the strategic plan becomes a vehicle for institutional progress.

Implementation Plans

Implementation plans detail the activities the institution will undertake to accomplish the objectives of its strategic plan. An implementation plan should be developed for each individual objective to identify who will do what throughout the time period the objective is being pursued. The format of implementation plans may vary in different institutions, but they should define three key elements: owner, action, and timeline.

Owner

As governance transitions from developing the strategic plan to implementing strategic planning, the number of participants will likely increase. Defining ownership is essential to fostering accountability throughout all levels of the institution. Museum executives may be assigned specific strategic plan goals that align with their role in the museum. The leaders of offices or divisions below those executives can then be assigned specific objectives that contribute to that goal. In our folk art museum example, the executive in charge of programming would be assigned the audience engagement goal and the director of museum experience would be assigned the visitor satisfaction objective.

Not all objectives of the strategic plan will have clear ownership. Perhaps an objective sets out a new line of effort that must be assigned to an owner as a new responsibility. Other objectives may need to be split into multiple parts because several offices will own a portion of the implementation planning. In our folk art museum example, the objective of increasing visitor satisfaction ratings may involve multiple lines of effort. Programs, facilities, and IT may each have roles to play in adding interactive exhibit features, while programs and visitor services may work together on creating multimedia guides. Each of these outcomes requires its own implementation planning with clear ownership of actions to achieve them.

Those assigned as owners will be responsible for preparing and carrying out the associated actions. These assignments should not come as a surprise to these leaders and their staff. An institution that is smartly incorporating the lessons from the change management building block of FIRM will have already consulted with many of them during the development process. Strategic planning benefits from the early investment of time to share insights both during development and once the strategic plan has been finalized.

Actions

The owner makes a list of all the actions needed to move from the current state to the future state articulated in the objective. These actions may not be very detailed at first, especially actions that will occur further in the future and may change based on the results of earlier actions. By treating the implementation plan as a living document, owners will be able to develop and refine the list of actions as the pathway to the objective becomes clearer.

Continuing our folk art museum example, the offices working together on the interactive exhibits and multimedia guides should make a detailed list of the actions needed to complete these efforts. Perhaps they need to hold workshops with staff for design and planning, purchase new technology, and hire a consultant with expertise the museum currently lacks. By breaking down efforts into the most detailed actions currently known, ownership will become clearer as will the associated resource needs.

Timeline

Time is certainly a resource that can limit progress toward an objective. Because objectives should already include a time component (three years in our visitor satisfaction example), timelines at the implementation plan level should be specific to each action. Timelines will require owners to make a lot of assumptions about available staff and financial resources and any related actions required from their museum colleagues.

Continuing our example, the team of owners drafting the actions associated with interactive exhibits may realize that some of their plans would require changes to the facility that would take more than three years to complete. Perhaps they scale back the interactive elements to those that would require minimal alterations to the museum building, yet still markedly improve visitor experience. Alternatively, they could take the proposal to the governance body to determine if this is an investment the museum wants to make in its pursuit of the strategic goal of improving visitor engagement.

Monitoring

While the strategic plan itself is a document that endures throughout its established lifetime, implementation plans are living documents. Owners should regularly monitor them for progress and revise them to reflect the latest planned actions. Strategic planning governance should establish a regular cadence for owners to brief their implementation plan performance.

Governance should track accomplishment of actions or milestones in the plan, assess the impact of delays, and address resource constraints. The executive responsible for each goal should oversee monitoring of all the implementation plans beneath it, with key information elevated to institution-wide strategic planning governance. Governance should establish monitoring processes across appropriate levels of leadership at quarterly, biannual, and annual frequencies.

In our folk art museum example, the owners of the actions in the visitor satisfaction implementation plan would need to report on their progress each quarter to the programming executive responsible for the broader goal. The executive may require the owners to make biannual updates to their implementation plans to keep up with changing conditions. At the end of each year, the executive can summarize the progress toward the overall goal and objective in a report to the highest level of governance. The report should reference key actions and milestones accomplished in the implementation plans and quantify progress toward the three-year objective of a 15 percent increase in visitor satisfaction.

Perhaps at the end of year one the visitor satisfaction survey shows an increase of 5 percent. Governance may be very pleased by this result, as it demonstrates they are one-third of the way to their objective in one-third of the time. However, measuring successful performance is not always that simple.

Instead, imagine the survey increased only 2 percent in the first year. Drawing on the details of the implementation plans, the executive may advise governance that they are not concerned by this slow start. Much of the first year was spent getting funding, staffing, and contracts in place, so visitor-facing outcomes are not expected until years two and three. Not wanting to wait a full year to find out, governance may ask the executive to brief again in six months so they can more closely monitor visitor satisfaction performance in the critical second year.

Failure to regularly track performance data will hamper the success of an institution's strategic plan. Governance oversight of implementation plan progress ensures accountability toward the aims of the strategic plan. Without this connection, a museum will find that its strategic plan has reached the end of its lifecycle, yet many of its objectives remain incomplete.

FIRM CONNECTION: BUDGETING

The FIRM approach requires integration of strategic planning into the budget cycle. Implementation plans are the most detailed part of strategic planning, but they span across multi-year objectives. Budget formulation becomes the forum to give implementation plan actions the resources they need for the upcoming year. This annual process ensures that a museum prioritizes its activities and aligns its resources based on its strategic plan priorities.

Prioritization

A strategic plan will direct an institution toward a handful of goals, each with multiple objectives and cascading implementation plans. This creates a very long to-do list. It would be impossible for a museum to begin implementing every objective on the day the strategic plan is launched. No matter how committed an institution is to executing its strategic plan, no one can do everything all at once.

Launching a strategic plan does not magically conjure the staff, funding, and relationships needed to carry it out. Funds must be raised, new staff hired, and contracts put in place before any real progress can be made. Individually these tasks are time-consuming, but collectively they can take up a significant part of the timelines associated with implementing a strategic plan. Not only must an implementation plan owner consider what capacity they must build to contribute to the larger goal, but the institution's overall capacity for simultaneously fundraising, hiring, and contracting on multiple fronts will also have its limits.

Offices will expect additional resources to tackle new or expanded initiatives that stem from the strategic plan. Employees will feel overwhelmed by the prospect of adding more work to their already full plates. Human resources and procurement will be flooded with requests for new hiring and contracting actions. An institution that fails to organize activities across the many parts of its strategic plan implementation will find that all activities begin to stall. If everything is treated as an urgent priority, then nothing is truly a priority.

A key component of integrating strategic planning and budgeting is priority setting. Strategic planning governance must make difficult decisions to guide implementation of the strategic plan and ensure that those decisions are carried forward in the annual budget. The initial work on implementation plans can provide a feedback loop to aid this decision-making.

An implementation plan should outline not just the substantive work that will be carried out, but any preceding actions that are needed to prepare for this work. The owner may estimate the amount of time needed to develop a fundraising proposal and hire new staff. The implementation plan can note the interdependencies in these actions: perhaps initial work on job descriptions and hiring announcements can begin before funds are raised, but it would be unwise to make a job offer until the development office has secured at least some funds to pay the person's salary.

Reviewing the first round of implementation plans can help strategic planning governance understand how much lead time each line of effort may need and make decisions about where to direct finite resources first. There are many ways to think about pacing strategic priorities. Governance may determine that $1 million is available in the upcoming year to give a jump start to certain lines of work while fundraising for other efforts catches up. Perhaps they divide implementation into multiple tranches based on how many hiring actions human resources can pursue at one time.

Prioritization is not just about adding resources—it also requires subtracting. The existence of a strategic plan does not entitle an institution to unlimited growth. All the work in support of the strategic plan must be done with existing resources, at least until more resources can be added. Existing work occupies staff time and financial resources that could otherwise be redirected to pursue strategic priorities. It is essential that new work to support the strategic plan is not viewed in a vacuum.

A museum that has thoughtfully prepared a strategic plan that is not merely a reflection of what it already does will necessarily find that some ongoing activities do not fit within its strategic goals. The alignment of ongoing activities is hardest at the beginning of strategic plan implementation and needs to be continually reevaluated to ensure the museum hasn't veered off course as implementation plans are better defined.

During the years a museum is implementing its strategic plan, new work may be presented to a museum by external stakeholders. Perhaps another institution or government agency proposes a partnership with the museum. A donor may offer a large sum for a specific project they would like the museum to take on. When these opportunities arise, strategic planning governance should be convened to consider whether these new areas of work would steer resources away from the strategic plan. Even those opportunities that come with dedicated funding will still require oversight and staff time, creating additional projects to be managed. Governance may recommend further discussions with the potential partners or donors to bring the scope of the work more in line with the institution's direction, or the opportunities may need to be declined.

These decisions are certainly difficult for governance members to make, but also very difficult for subordinate leaders and employees to receive. While prioritization is a necessary reality, the language of prioritization can seem harsh. Stating that a project is not a priority to receive resources can be very personal for an employee who has invested significant effort in the work. Strategic plan implementation requires cultural change that will involve all levels of staff across the institution. Change management and communication are important to help staff understand the strategic decisions that underpin priority setting. Communicating with staff about what the priorities are will also help them understand de-prioritization. Sharing timelines and explaining why the museum cannot do everything all at once will add context to the ongoing strategic planning activities.

Resourcing

Prioritization is not merely a time-management strategy (which task will I do first?), but a recognition of limited resources (how should I distribute my finite resources?). Linking strategy to budget is about ensuring the institution is putting its money where its priorities are. A museum that seeks to implement its strategic plan by adding new strategic priorities on top of all existing spending would need to have extraordinarily strong finances to support such rapid growth.

Too often, leaders attempt to soften the blow of prioritization by not directly stating what is a low priority, only what is a high priority. The notion is that by raising a few items to the top of the pile, leaders are still communicating what they want the institution to be focused on while minimizing discomfort and disruption. However, unless an institution is blessed with plentiful resources, these leaders will be unable to fully pursue their priorities without making difficult decisions.

At the same time, prioritization should not be taken to simply mean a list of priorities. It does not require itemizing every project and activity within a museum and putting them in rank order. This would be a difficult undertaking because not all work is created equal or can be easily compared across categories. A simple ranking would assume that everything below a certain line (representing available funding) would simply be cut. However, institutions aren't only made of discrete and severable projects that would not affect the overall operation of the museum. A ranking approach would also not take into account the reality that work has progressed to different stages in each effort listed. A museum would be ill-advised to halt a project that is a month from completion because another project has been designated a higher priority. So how does a museum actually go about setting and resourcing priorities?

The act of prioritization must be carried out through a repeatable and recordable process. Luckily, a museum that has built a robust budgeting process under FIRM already has the framework in place to which these strategic planning considerations can be added. The time to evaluate strategic planning priorities comes at the start of the budget cycle, when budget formulation guidance is being distributed. The budget playbook can be updated to set aside specific time for budget owners to undertake this strategic activity before they put pen to paper on their draft spending plans.

Prioritization begins with the question of what activities to start, stop, or continue to work on across the museum. This approach provides clear pathways for budget owners to choose from based on the facts of each unique body of work. Let us first examine the activities that may fall into the "stop" or "continue" categories. These are areas of work the institution was already carrying out in the prior budget year. Starting with a copy of last year's budget, the budget owner is asked to identify which areas of work they expect to stop or continue in the upcoming year. Activities that stop may include one-time budget needs that will not recur or projects that will naturally come to their conclusion before the new year. Activities that continue may include unfinished projects as well as operational functions that are needed regardless of which projects the office pursues. The budget owner may be surprised to find that they want to continue nearly all of their activities and only limited funds would be freed up by the few activities that were marked to be stopped.

This is where the "start" category comes in. Setting aside the prior year budget, budget formulation guidance should prompt budget owners to review their implementation plans and assign resources for the upcoming year based on the progress they seek. Both funds and personnel should be assigned as if no other work is occupying them. This will keep budget owners focused on strategic priorities.

Comparing these two exercises (the stop/continue list and the start list) can help signal to the budget owner where lower priorities or other legacy work may be taking up precious resources needed to progress in their implementation plans. The budget owner can then take another pass at both lists in an effort to marry the two together within the resource levels prescribed in budget formulation guidance. This process will not be easy. The most important area of focus is how to shift resources from the "continue" list to the "stop" list.

Imagine that during implementation planning, an owner recognizes that current staff are unable to take on the additional work required with all the other work streams currently

Figure 4.2 Start, Stop, or Continue. *Source*: Ashley Amos.

ongoing. Their solution to this problem may be to request more staff in their implementation plan, enabling them to use current staff to continue existing work and hire new staff for the new work. This approach assumes that the existing work and the strategic priority are equally important and that enough resources exist to pursue both. But that is rarely the case.

The start, stop, and continue exercise provides several options to address the limited resources. If the budget owner knows that the ongoing project is planned to wrap up in one year, they may recommend that implementation be delayed until the employees are available for reassignment. This recommendation is further strengthened if a donor has already directed a restricted gift to the ongoing project that has not been fully spent. Deferral of the strategic priority would need to be approved by governance and reflected in an updated timeline in the implementation plan. For example, if the implementation plan previously assumed it would take four months to hire new personnel, waiting one year to leverage existing personnel instead would result in implementation starting eight months later than originally planned. This approach puts the existing project on the "continue" list, but with an established transition plan to shift resources to the strategic priority.

Alternatively, imagine the ongoing work is not tied to a specific outcome or end date. It is common that activities considered core to an office began as well-defined projects that have continually expanded in scope since their original conception. Engaging in a strategy-to-budget process forces the budget owners to grapple with the difficult questions of whether and how to identify an off-ramp for these engrained activities so they can pursue other work. Perhaps the budget owner is not able to sufficiently justify the continuation of this work and governance decides that it should be discontinued. The budget owner would be directed to prepare a plan to wrap up the work as soon as possible and redirect existing staff to support the strategic priority. This approach places the ongoing work on the "stop" list and allows the strategic priority to be added to the "start" list in the upcoming budget.

During this process, budget owners will likely need support from their senior leaders or facilitators to help stimulate thinking and challenge assumptions. Budget and strategic planning governance will need to be engaged when decisions cannot be made and require elevation. An institution that is early in the process of establishing a strategy-to-budget connection may require a formal governance review for all museum budget owners before budget formulation can proceed. This early engagement of governance can help validate individual decisions and ensure consistency of approach across the institution.

When a budget owner has outlined an achievable list of work to start, stop, and continue in the upcoming year, they can begin populating their spending plan with specific line items and cost estimates. When completed spend plans are provided to the finance office for review by budget governance, the updated budget cycle should also account for coordination with strategic planning governance.

Strategic planning and budgeting governance structures must become formally interconnected. Creating this link sends an important message throughout the museum that strategy drives resource decisions. To the extent that governance participants in the two bodies overlap, they must look at decisions through both strategy and budget lenses and document choices made across the institution. The strategy-to-budget connection also benefits the museum in dealings with its board and donors. Budget assumptions that increase either sources or uses will be strengthened by demonstrating how the budget growth is in pursuit of strategic priorities.

Strategic priorities that are not approved for resources in budget formulation need to be revised in their implementation planning. An action may need to be scaled back or a timeline shifted. Strategic priorities that exceed available resources must continue to be evaluated against ongoing work in future years' start, stop, and continue exercises. As this cycle repeats, fundraising based on the strategic plan will have an opportunity to deliver new funding sources that may allow the institution to expand into new work with fewer reductions elsewhere.

FIRM CONNECTIONS

As an individual exercise, a strategic plan has a unique ability to align all the offices within a museum in a shared direction. The value of a strategic plan is magnified when the strategic planning process is leveraged as an Integration building block of FIRM. Strategic planning is closely linked to budgeting because together these building blocks guide and resource an integrated set of institutional priorities.

The institutional benefits of strategic planning are further strengthened through the application of governance and change management—the two remaining building blocks that form the Integration pillar. The FIRM approach ensures that employees are not left in the dark about how the institution's priorities will change with a new strategic plan. Decisions are made through a defined governance structure, not behind closed doors or as one-offs. The strategic plan drives the budget decisions that make strategic objectives achievable.

Developing and implementing a strategic plan in the context of FIRM sharpens a museum's ability to direct the full weight of institutional effort toward its aims. By the time our fictional folk art museum is ready to draft its next strategic plan, it will find itself in a different place than the last time it undertook this exercise. The museum will reflect on its mission and vision and contemplate what new heights it could reach in the coming years.

Chapter 5

Governance

INTEGRATION BUILDING BLOCK 3

The next building block in the Integration pillar is governance. Governance is critical to the ability of an institution to establish and maintain the strategy-to-budget connection. Governance ensures that cross-institutional perspectives guide the development of strategic plans and budgets and provides a forum for decision-making. The implementation of strategic plans and the execution of the budget are two sides of the same coin. The application of governance to the range of cross-functional projects and processes within a museum can further deepen integration, fostering a more efficient, effective, and transparent institution.

We have all worked on important projects either within our office or as a member of a cross-functional team. Many have gone well, but those that have gone sideways tend to stick with us. These poorly planned projects may have been bogged down by disagreements in approach, personality conflicts, and or an inability to make a decision. Perhaps curators and historians were unable to agree on how a particular artifact should be presented to the public. The specific challenges will vary but it begs the question of whether there are any commonalities between these failed projects.

We have all worked on a particular project where our boss did not clearly articulate the intent of the project. When this happens, an assembled team may run with its own project without considering the entire institution. An example of this could be if the museum marketing team was tasked to start a media campaign to spur interest in the museum, but did not reach out to colleagues outside of their office. In this case, they did not coordinate with the curators to see if they were working on an exhibit that would attract new visitors.

There are many decision points that need to be sorted out in an organized manner before a project even starts. Then, there will be many more decision points along the way during the project's implementation. Consider the example of a new financial system. This would seem like a clearcut project because it is owned by the finance office. However, perhaps the finance office does not consider the IT office equities in selecting a new system to connect to the museum's internal network. Perhaps system users throughout the museum were not considered when the project was being developed, only the needs of the finance office staff. Perhaps the project fell victim to the other extreme: too many system users were asked to participate in the project. No mechanism existed to triage numerous system requirements from different stakeholders, and the software developers were unsure of which requirements to implement.

As the project got underway, there was no distinction between priorities. Roles were not defined and no one had any authority to greenlight or say no to any project proposals. The project team established regular meetings, but without clear agendas the discussions would digress into unresolved debates. These failures create a lack of trust and prevent the project team from working together effectively. Lack of accountability among the participants led to finger pointing. The project would never be finished; it would always be in development.

These project examples had one thing in common. They each were missing a clearly articulated governance structure. Governance provides a path to decision-making related to a specific project or activity of the institution. Before we detail what activity-based governance contributes to FIRM, it is necessary to distinguish it from the institutional governance that is already in place at any museum. Activity-based governance is designed to be complementary to and fill in the gaps within institutional governance for decisions that do not need to include the entire institutional hierarchy.

INSTITUTIONAL GOVERNANCE

Institutional governance frameworks of a museum are established at the time of their founding. These designated roles and responsibilities are essential for organizational stability. Museums leverage governance structures for many reasons that will impact a range of museum priorities. These include upholding donor trust, optimizing resource allocation, and achieving mission-driven outcomes.

Institutional governance provides the mechanism to determine who is making strategic decisions for the institution. This governance is established through external boards and committees as well as internal leadership hierarchy under the museum director. These structures may be documented through an institutional charter or legislative authorization. Governing documents detail how decisions are made and how they will be communicated to the museum community.

This model is often entrenched in tradition and stability, aiming to provide a clear framework for managing operations and resolving conflicts. Key features of institutional governance include centralized decision-making, standardized procedures, and a top-down flow of authority and communication.

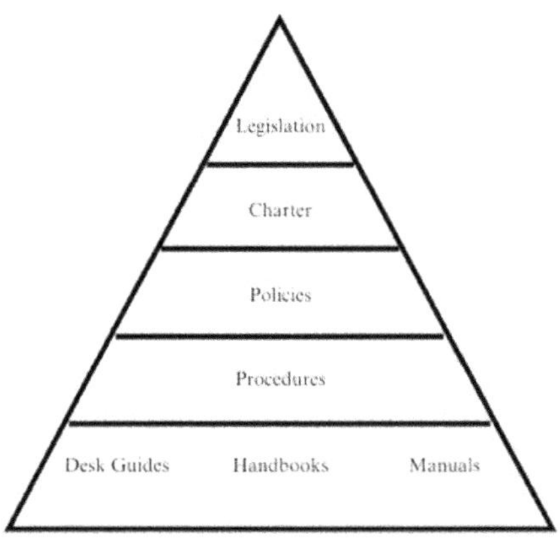

Figure 5.1 Governing Documents at Different Levels of the Institution. *Source*: Ashley Amos.

Leaders distribute instructions and guidance down their respective branches of the hierarchy and employees propose actions up through their leadership chain. Many decisions can be made through these structures when the decisions are confined to one branch of an organizational chart, but what happens when issues arise that cut across multiple parts of the museum? The solution offered by institutional governance is to take that issue all the way up to the point in the hierarchy where the affected branches connect at a single leader who can serve as the decision-maker.

Institutional governance has its limitations. This hierarchical nature of management doesn't usually evolve easily. Changes to the size and structure of the museum, development in its culture, or variability in available resources can test institutional governance. The formality and centralization of the structure may not be nimble enough to respond to particular challenges or manage multiple portfolios of work.

As a museum matures, crosscutting governance becomes necessary for success. As this happens, the museum must adapt and develop a framework to solve diverse problems. Reliance on formal structures can sometimes lead to rigidity and resistance to change. This will hinder adaptability in dynamic environments. The ability to quickly respond to unexpected

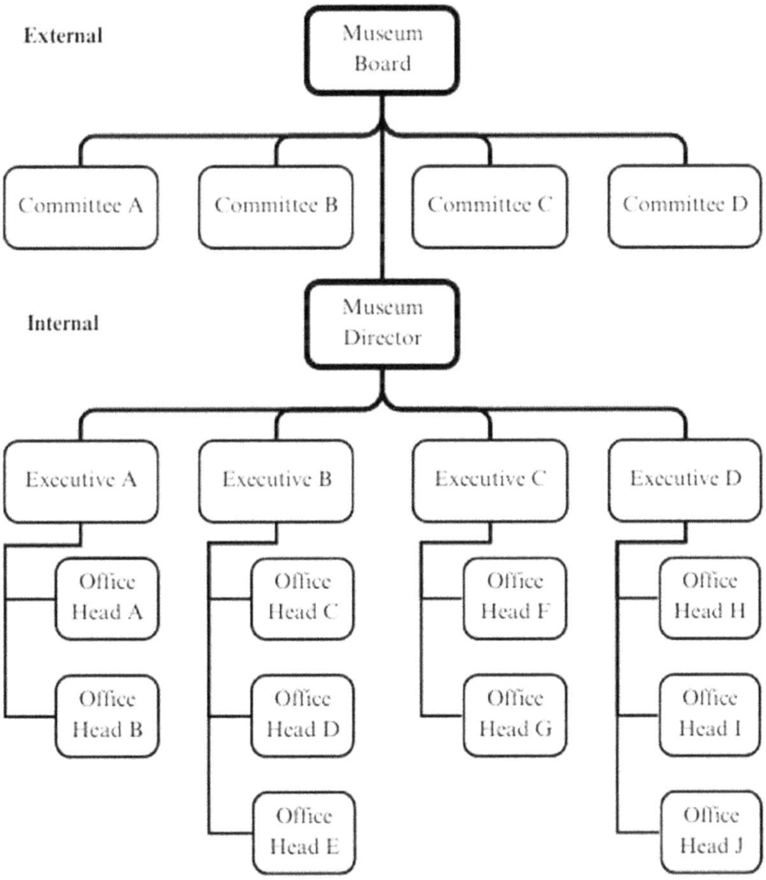

Figure 5.2 Institutional Governance Using Museum Hierarchy. *Source*: Ashley Amos.

events and make decisions may be slow to implement due to long-standing and entrenched processes.

In many cases, innovation may be stifled as individuals adhere strictly to established norms rather than exploring new ideas. Diversity of thought suffers when every problem is solved with the same approach by the same set of employees. Systemic resistance, silos, and long-standing power structures need to be broken down. These silos have been strengthened overtime because of the stability offered by the institutional governance model.

Institutional governance and governing documents have become entrenched when museum policy and procedures are standing in the way of addressing new problems, rather than being considered for adaptation to help the museum better address challenges that arise. The good news is that institutional governance does not need to be thrown out the window to overcome these hurdles. Governance can be augmented at the activity level to address new needs that arise as a museum advances.

ACTIVITY-BASED GOVERNANCE

Throughout this book, we use the term governance to refer to the structure—at the activity level—that a museum will put in place to ensure that decisions are carried through on crosscutting processes or activities. Activity-based governance is a management approach that prioritizes decision-making and accountability based on specific activities within a museum. Activity-based governance is unlike traditional hierarchical models which rely on centralized authority and formal structures.

In FIRM, an activity can be a process or project that requires governance. An activity can be a short-lived project like creation of a traveling exhibit. This activity will have a clear start and end date determined by the project. An activity can also be long term like the establishment of a digital steering committee (DSC) that will become part of the fabric of how the museum operates. In particular, the budgeting, strategic planning, and risk management building blocks of FIRM rely on the creation of activity-based governance to provide clear guidance, communication, and decision structures to support these ongoing processes.

Let us suppose that a museum wants to build a traveling exhibit to tour college campuses. In the current organizational chart, exhibits would be under the jurisdiction of the chief curator. However, leadership has determined that this project's primary focus is on accessibility and creating new partnerships. Because this project is traveling to campuses, outside the walls of the museum, the director determines that the appropriate leader for this project is the head of campus outreach. The development of the exhibit will be just one phase of the project, with a second phase ongoing while the exhibit is touring the country. The chief curator will be a critical member of the project team in phase one, but will not continue to be involved in phase two.

By linking decision-making directly to specific outcomes and promoting a sense of ownership among stakeholders, activity-based governance fosters a more dynamic and efficient organizational culture. Institutional governance and activity-based governance represent opposite sides of the same coin, each with its own benefits and challenges. The two forms of governance are not mutually exclusive. They are parts of a whole that create an organizational ecosystem supported by the building blocks of FIRM. The short- and long-term projects fostered under the activity-based approach add a level of support to the institution by filling in organizational gaps. The vertical institutional hierarchy is enhanced by cross-cutting opportunities to strengthen the museum with new connection points.

Museums, like all well-established institutions, will instinctively default to their hierarchical structure. This form of vertical management exists where decision-making authority and responsibility flow from top-level management downward through various levels of an organization or government. Activity-based governance will be flatter. Decision-making authority and responsibilities are shared across different departments, teams, or stakeholders. This focus on the horizontal relationships rather than the vertical ones helps right-size governance for the problem at hand.

For example, the head of IT security wants to change how often the museum's servers are patched to be in sync with their cloud service provider. At first glance, this decision seems to be internal to the IT office and a vertical approach would suffice, requiring approval through the executive overseeing IT security. However, program staff and even visitors may be impacted by information and systems undergoing the new patch cycle. Casting a wide horizontal net that pulls together a committee reflective of the entire organizational chart would be unruly and unhelpful.

In this scenario, the head of IT security establishes a change control board to approve and schedule system upgrades and patches. This group is responsible for reviewing, evaluating, approving, and managing changes to an IT project or system. It consists of stakeholders from various relevant areas such as project management, systems development, operations, information security, and representative end users or customers. The various perspectives represented on this board will ensure that changes are thoroughly considered, planned, and carried out, minimizing risks and disruptions while maximizing the benefits of changes to projects or systems.

By making this board cross-functional and including representatives of key impacted stakeholders, these changes can be processed and memorialized through the appropriate policies and procedures. The board structure can be maintained not just for this change, but for future IT events that need consultation and coordination. This governance structure helps maintain consistency, stability, and alignment with project objectives throughout the change process.

CREATING A CHARTER

Establishing a new activity-based governance structure begins with the charter. This should not be confused with the charter that established the museum. A museum charter is a formal document that establishes the existence and purpose of the institution. This broader document outlines the museum's mission and operational structure. It serves as a foundational document that defines the framework within which the museum operates and provides guidance on its strategic direction.

The charter is often created at the inception of the institution but can be revised or updated as the museum evolves. It serves as a reference point for stakeholders, including employees, management, donors, and external parties, to understand the museum's purpose and how it operates.

The same guidance provided by a museum charter can be applied to a project or process using activity-based governance. This charter brings the lessons of the institutional charter to the activity level. Institutional norms are leveraged to create alignment among team members from different reporting authorities. By disengaging from the organizational structure, the

Table 5.1 Elements of a Charter

Elements of a charter
• Authority & Scope • Membership • Operating Procedures • Accountability & Oversight

Source: Ashley Amos.

project team frees itself from existing silos and engages a cross-section of the museum selected for their shared equities in the activity.

The following example illustrates how a charter can help establish and document activity-based governance.

Authority and Scope

The charter should include the authority that allows the group to operate. It will also detail what responsibility the group will have over its particular discipline. The charter should include an amendment process for amending the governance charter itself, typically requiring approval from designated stakeholders. The authority to operate this governance structure should have a conclusion date if the project or activity is not intended to exist for an indefinite time period. The governance can sunset when the project is complete and be reinstituted when and if necessary. It can also be extended if the source of authority deems it necessary.

The scope is a description of the activity that the governance body will oversee. This activity needs to be uniquely held by the governance structure, or else the museum risks tasking multiple offices or bodies with overlapping scope.

Let us assume a museum's Chief Information Officer (CIO) is formally given the authority by the director to convene a crosscutting digital steering committee (DSC). This group will be charged with creating a digital strategy with the express purpose of prioritizing future digital investments. The DSC will evaluate digital problems statements and proposals from museum offices. The intent of this evaluation role is to ensure that future digital projects include a roadmap with proposed timelines, a clear understanding of budget impact, and a justification of how they fit with the current IT priorities in the strategic plan. The DSC will operate for a term of two years, with an option to extend, based on a review of committee accomplishments by the museum director.

Membership

The charter includes a description of the roles and responsibilities of the members of the group. The charter also outlines how members are selected and transitioned in and out of the group. Members of a decision body for an activity include roles such as a chair and committee members. The charter may specify that the museum director appoints the chair and the chair appoints all other members.

Activity-based governance roles should not be confused with project management roles. Project management is the application of knowledge, skills, tools, and techniques to project activities to meet project requirements.[1] It is the practice of planning, organizing, and executing the tasks into a product, service, or deliverable. Project management functions will be carried out by a working-level structure including roles such as project lead, project manager, core team members, and consulted experts. Governance sits above these project management operations to make strategic-level decisions that helps the project remain on course.

In our example, the museum director designates the CIO as DSC chair, with the governance authority to make the decisions on project implementation timelines and to submit recommendations for funding. The committee members would be office heads whose offices have a digital presence.

Before this committee was established, the available institutional governance forums to discuss these activities were insufficient. The CIO could present the issues at a regular convening of all the museum's office heads, but many did not have equities in their portfolio. Some participants would tune out of discussions, while others would ask tangential questions that would take the discussions off topic.

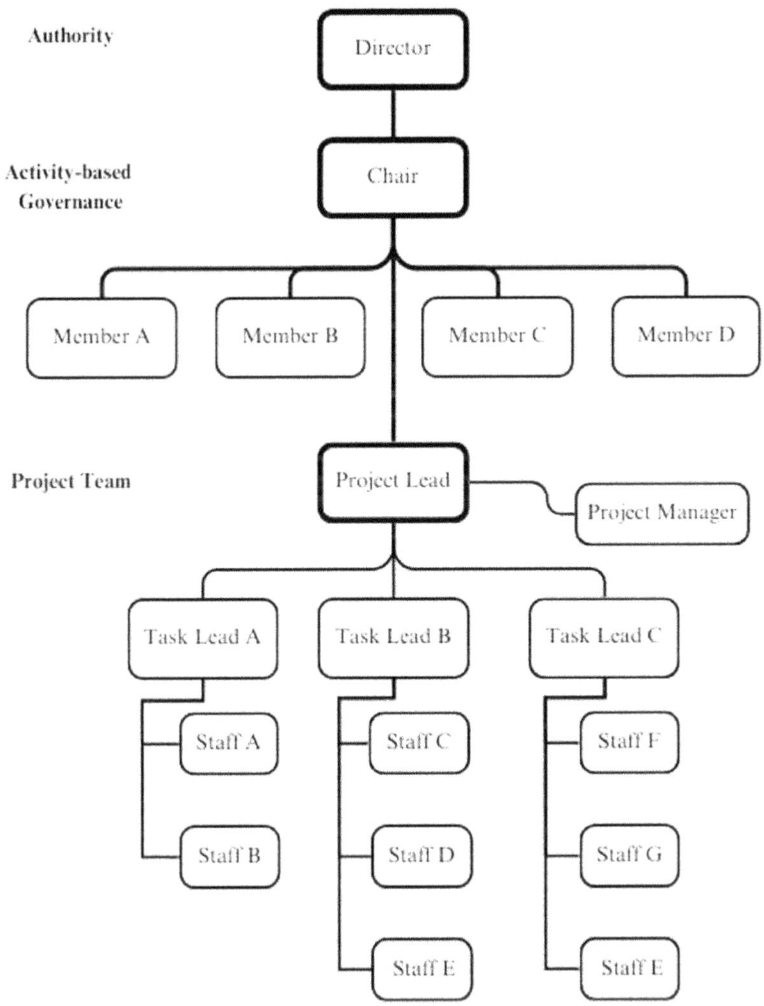

Figure 5.3 Activity-based Governance Providing Oversight of a Project. *Source*: Ashley Amos.

The CIO also previously elevated discussions to the museum's executive leadership group, which formed the most senior level of institutional governance in the museum. But they would often defer to the expertise of specific office heads who worked below them, prompting the CIO to have individual conversations with office heads on their particular equities.

With the charter defining the members of the DSC, the CIO now has clarity on who the institution has decided should be consulted on these matters.

Operating Procedures

The charter should outline the procedures that will govern the decision-making process, such as guidelines for scheduling and conducting meetings and requirements for reporting and communication with stakeholders.

Continuing with our example, the DSC charter establishes that the group meets on the first Monday of every month. A quorum of members must be present for the meeting to commence. One week prior to each meeting, an individual is assigned to prepare an agenda and distribute the minutes from the last meeting. The charter specifies the process for offices to submit digital proposals to the committee for consideration.

Let us suppose that the Chief Technology Officer (CTO) is working on a project to move the museum to a modern phone system that uses a cloud-based phone system and all services are managed offsite through the internet rather than using traditional phone lines. The CTO convenes a project team to draft a project proposal for the DSC. The DSC approves this project to move forward. Because this project has a budget impact (purchasing and installing the new phone system), the DSC charter requires that the project must next be submitted through the museum's budgeting process, adding another governance perspective to the decision. If instead the project was one that could be carried out within existing resources, the charter would allow the approved project to be immediately added to the DSC's digital roadmap. A project that is denied is placed in the committee archives.

All projects that are approved or denied in the DSC meeting are designated to be published on the museum's intranet site no later than one week after the meeting. Making the key decisions and reports accessible to the museum community increases transparency and improves understanding within the museum community of how to engage with the governance process. The digital roadmap allows the DSC to monitor progress on all approved projects through completion.

Accountability and Oversight

The charter should include mechanisms for ensuring accountability and oversight. This will ensure that these new committees do not become disconnected from the rest of the institution.

Our DSC example works in concert with other governance structures within the museum. For DSC projects that require funding, they will need to be considered as part of the annual budget formulation process which is approved by the museum's budgeting governance. For projects that require no funding but the coordination of colleagues in the IT office, the aforementioned change control board will provide internal coordination.

The DSC may also have scheduled engagements with the museum's institutional governance. The chair may provide quarterly progress reports to the museum director and executive leadership team and present the latest version on the digital roadmap at the annual meeting of the museum's external board.

MAINTAINING GOVERNANCE

Now that the museum is embracing a new way of doing business, maintaining this new framework is paramount. Working closely with stakeholders ensures that all relevant parties are aware of the charter and operating in accordance with its contents. This communication keeps the governance structure aligned with the needs and expectations of an ever-changing museum.

When a museum implements this part of FIRM, it will have to ensure that any resistance to new governance is addressed. Employees may instinctively revert to the organizational hierarchy rather than using the new governance structure to gain approval. Others may go to the museum director to ask that they overrule a denial by governance. All leaders in the museum must commit to the charter for new governance frameworks and make sure they are appropriately communicated.

Looking at our example of the DSC, museum leadership should not promote or provide funding for digital projects without approval from the DSC. Budget and procurement policies should be written that require documentation of DSC approval before investments budget authority is provided and purchases are made. If a museum leader presents a digital project for funding during budget formulation without a recommendation from the DSC, this request should not be approved.

Amending the Charter

Amending an activity charter may be necessary to ensure that the governance remains relevant to the activities it is intended to support. A museum is not a static entity. Internal and external factors will change how the museum operates over time. In many cases these changes are organic in nature. Museums are becoming more complex and diversified. New restricted donations may fundamentally change what the museum presents to the public. A new director may implement a new strategic plan, changing roles and responsibilities of office heads throughout the museum. Any of these examples could require a modification to governance charters.

Continuing with the example of the DSC charter, after two years during its scheduled review the museum director determines that the DSC is approving projects that require too many distinct and incompatible software platforms. The CIO reports that the museum doesn't have a policy on software approval. Therefore, project leads were all selecting different software solutions for their individual project needs. This was not out of policy and therefore could not be considered as a reason to deny a project request. At this point, the director amends the charter to require the DSC to catalog all the museum's software platforms and to consider whether existing software can support new digital projects before the procurement of a new product is approved.

FIRM CONNECTIONS

The building blocks of FIRM are designed to work together, and implementation of each block can and should happen at its own pace, specific to the internal and external factors at each museum. Activity-based governance is all about the ability for a museum to make decisions when employees have to work across boundaries. Leadership can encourage the formation of cross-functional decision-making bodies that bring together diverse perspectives and expertise to make strategic decisions.

Chapter 6

Change Management

INTEGRATION BUILDING BLOCK 4

The final building block of the Integration pillar is change management. Constructing the pillars of FIRM puts an institution in a constant state of motion. Roles, structures, and processes will be changing. But these are just the changes to the organization. Any effort to advance an institution's financial well-being will also ask people to change their behavior. Change management considers how to navigate both the organizational and behavioral aspects of change. Structured approaches to change can help an institution transition from its current state to a desired future state by minimizing disruption and maximizing the likelihood of success. Like governance, the application of change management enables a museum to move as one integrated unit, ensuring that parts of the institution are not left behind or disregarded as the museum advances.

This chapter focuses primarily on the behavioral aspect of change, which is too often left behind when the institution's focus is on the organizational mechanics of change. The strategies in this chapter should be paired with the best practices outlined in other chapters to create a full picture of how change management can be applied in support of all the building blocks of FIRM.

We cannot underestimate the value of participation in effecting change. Directive, hierarchical management styles may simply order employees to do things differently. Employees facing the uncertainty of change may resist if they feel they are being strong-armed into changes they don't fully understand. Change management focuses on getting the people affected by change to understand, support, and eventually even champion the change. This behavior-centered approach is especially conducive to a museum environment where values tend toward evidence-based analysis and consensus building.

Change management is often only applied concurrent with the change itself: for example, when a new strategic plan is released. In the days leading up to the release, drafters will prepare multiple means of communication—staff meetings, emails, posters, videos, and town halls—designed to introduce the new document and explain what it means for the institution. However, this limited view of change management does too little too late to quell the fears that accompany change.

Change management should begin as soon as the need for change has been identified. No one individual can make organizational changes alone, so other stakeholders need to be brought in on the idea as it begins to take shape. As soon as these early conversations begin, the cat is out of the bag.

Continuing with our example of the new strategic plan, it is very likely that many employees have been aware that strategic plan development was underway for months. Perhaps an employee saw strategic planning governance meetings on their boss's calendar. Another employee was involved in contracting for the strategic planning facilitator. Word spreads and soon the entire museum is abuzz: How will it affect me? Is my work going to be valued? Why are we talking about this now when there are so many other things to do?

Failure to address concerns long before the strategic plan is finalized merely allows them to fester. Further, this approach misses important opportunities to bring more people into the change. As we discussed in the strategic planning chapter, early involvement of employees and stakeholders at many levels not only familiarizes them with what is coming but also allows the resulting strategic plan to benefit from diverse perspectives.

Another way to ensure a change effort fails comes after the change has been introduced. The change management mindset is switched off as soon as the strategic plan has been successfully rolled out. This approach virtually guarantees that the document will be filed away and forgotten, or at the very least given lip service by employees that go through the motions of documenting how their work supports the strategic plan.

The ultimate goal of managing change is to ensure that change sticks. All that work would be for nothing if the strategic plan does not become a true guidepost for the institution that is ingrained in its culture. This is why the strategic plan *document* must lead to a strategic planning *process*. Ongoing governance, implementation planning, prioritization, and budgeting discussed in the strategic planning chapter are all change management tools designed to make the change stick. Without them, that strategic plan can easily be numbered among the estimated 70 percent of organizational changes that fail.[1]

TYPES OF CHANGE

While some may shortchange the change management process, the greatest mistake is to fail to apply change management at all. An example like a new strategic plan may seem like an obvious candidate for change management, but there are many types of change that an institution may need to manage.[2]

An institution will assume change management is needed when the scale of change will fundamentally transform the way it operates.[3] Perhaps this transformation is driven by external forces that the institution does not control: economic, political, social, or otherwise. Shifts in norms can prompt an institution to reexamine its place in the world and force it to adapt to survive.

Transformational changes may also be internally planned, especially in institutions with robust strategic planning and risk management processes that help them look to the future. Transformational changes that have strategic-level impacts across the entire institution may include a reorganization or mission expansion. For example, an act of Congress directed the National D-Day Museum in New Orleans to become the National World War II Museum.[4] The museum had to adapt to rapidly expand both its mission and its physical footprint just four years after opening.[5]

Smaller-scale changes may not feel worthy of all the effort of change management. These changes advance the institution along its current path.[6] Perhaps an existing process is being revised because some participants in the process have developed more efficient ways of operating. A policy loophole may have led to unintended consequences that require changes. Replacement of outdated software will impact user experience or have unfamiliar functionality.

What is common among these changes is that they are incremental in nature.[7] They may only represent slight changes from how things are currently done. However, it would be a mistake to simply drop these changes into employees' laps and assume they will adapt. Incremental changes may not require as robust of a change management process as transformational changes, but they will still be more likely to succeed if carried out with change management in mind from beginning to end.

Depending on how advanced an institution is when it begins adopting FIRM, the scale of changes needed may range from the incremental to the transformational. An institution embarking on strategic planning for the first time will need a transformational change mindset. By contrast, an institution with a long history of strategic planning may only seek to incrementally improve its process by strengthening its connections with annual budgeting. The former will have to invest significantly more energy in managing change compared to the latter. But both will benefit from applying the tenets of change management.

PARTICIPANTS IN CHANGE

Changemakers

Institutions don't change on their own. They are made up of people who make change happen. A change agent is a museum employee who identifies the need for a change and takes steps to enact that change. The change agent for transformational changes is likely to be the director or another executive leader. By virtue of their position and personality, this leader may be the right person to champion the change through the institutional gauntlet.

Change agents for incremental change can and should come from anywhere in the institution. They may not hold a fancy title or have broad responsibilities, but they see an opportunity to fix a problem or make an activity more efficient. They are able to clearly communicate the reasons behind the change, what needs to happen, and the expected outcomes to garner support from more powerful individuals who can serve as change sponsors.

The change sponsor is likely to be more senior than the change agent—perhaps their manager or office head—someone who can take the seed planted by the change agent and help it grow. They may be able to provide funding or authority that the change agent needs. Sponsors can help communicate and advocate at higher levels and across institutional boundaries. With the early support of a sponsor, even a more junior change agent can turn their idea into a full-fledged change project that far exceeds their individual reach.

Impacted Employees

Just as the faceless institution does not initiate change without changemakers, nor is the institution the target of change management. Institutions are made up of people. The institution only changes because the people impacted by the change decided to adopt it. The number of people impacted will depend on the nature and scope of the change. Incremental changes may be limited in impact to the role of a specific team or a process that involves multiple offices. Transformational changes may reach the entire institution with varying levels of impact to different offices, roles, and levels of the organizational hierarchy.

Inertia is a powerful force and people will continue doing things as they have been unless convinced otherwise. This is why people are so central to the process of change management. It requires identifying what stakeholders are necessary to participate in the change. Both individual and group dynamics come into play. Each person will have their own perspectives and opinions, and they will pay attention to how others around them are reacting to the change.

Impacted employees may negatively respond to change through both direct and indirect resistance. Direct resistance includes employees who openly object to the change or rally others against the change behind the scenes. These employees will cite the difficulty of the change as a reason why it will fail and should not be pursued.[8] Perhaps too many policies or procedures would need to change or too many offices would have to sign on. They will argue that the change will cost too much time or money.[9] They may say the change doesn't make sense for the museum by making the case that it runs contrary to institutional culture and history.[10] Or they may even deny there is a problem that needs fixing in the first place.

Indirect resistance occurs when employees stay silent while hoping the change effort will fall apart or stall out. They may appear to go along with the change while creating roadblocks or delays along the way. Perhaps they plan to quietly subvert the change by continuing to do things the old way.

Whether it manifests as direct or indirect resistance, impacted employees often resist for the common reasons. Some may feel threatened by the change. Others may lack confidence in their ability to adapt to the change. It is the job of the changemaker to identify the root of the resistance and build a counterpoint to each concern into their communication strategy.

A critical mass of support from impacted employees is needed to turn the tide in the changemaker's favor. Communication is integral to helping impacted employees understand their role and be actively engaged in managing change. Communication is not a one-time event but an ongoing and adaptive activity. Different stakeholders may require different types of communication. Messages can be tailored to resonate with various audiences, while considering their perspectives and needs. Two-way communication creates opportunities for feedback so concerns and suggestions are addressed. Diverse communication methods such as meetings, workshops, email, internal messaging channels, and the intranet help reach as many impacted employees as possible.

THE CHANGE MANAGEMENT LIFECYCLE

As discussed in the example of a strategic plan rollout, change management can be logically organized into three phases of effort: before, during, and after the change.[11]

In the first phase, the changemaker shakes up the status quo to prepare for change.[12] The changemaker has already identified the need for change, but now begins to build out the arguments for why the change is needed and how the change would benefit the institution. This is the time to develop an understanding of current behavior and begin to educate impacted employees about the benefits of the change.

The second phase is when the change is made.[13] This phase is not just the flip of a switch to implement the change. It continues to build on the momentum of phase one to understand employees, garner their support, and show them how to begin moving to the new behavior. The change occurs at a tipping point when the momentum has overcome the competing force

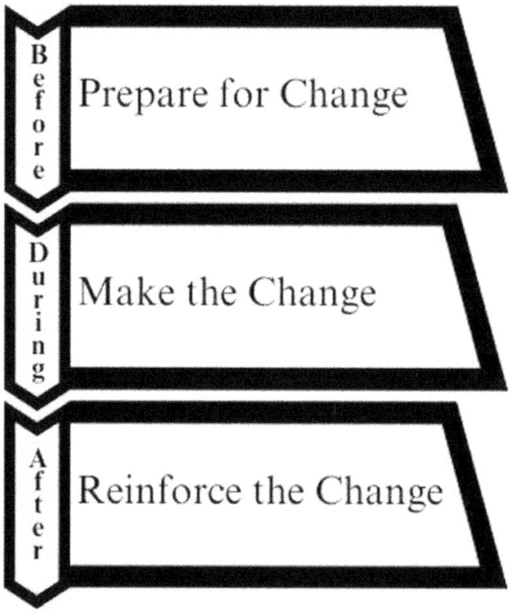

Figure 6.1 Phases of Change. *Source*: Ashley Amos.

of resistance. During the change, the changemaker continues pushing forward to prevent the support from retreating when there are bumps in the road.

The third phase aims to maintain the change by locking it in as the new status quo.[14] The change must be integrated into the institution's culture to ensure long-term sustainability and success. Impacted employees may have made it through the initial period of change, but may regress to the old way of doing things when other priorities move into the forefront. Changes to how an individual employee does their work can be reinforced through changes to group dynamics: governance structures, norms, policies, and processes help ensure each person fulfills their changed role as a participant within a larger ecosystem.

While the phases of change will follow the logical order of this sequence, how the phases operate is not so linear. Throughout each phase the changemaker is learning from and adapting to the environment. They must adopt an iterative approach to each phase, identifying areas where a change in tactics is needed to reach more participants where they are. Each phase should be carried out with a mindset of curiosity.

There are also necessary feedback loops between phases. The changemaker may have an initial plan for phases one through three, but each phase is subject to change based on what was learned in the previous phase. Adjusting each phase to build on the progress already made increases the likelihood that the change effort will have the desired outcome.

If these three phases seem like a simplistic way of describing change, worry not. Years of change management theory have further defined the steps that need to be taken to progress through the three general phases.[15] Throughout the remainder of this section, we will use the example of an institutional reorganization to illustrate how the phases and steps can be applied to a real-world change scenario.

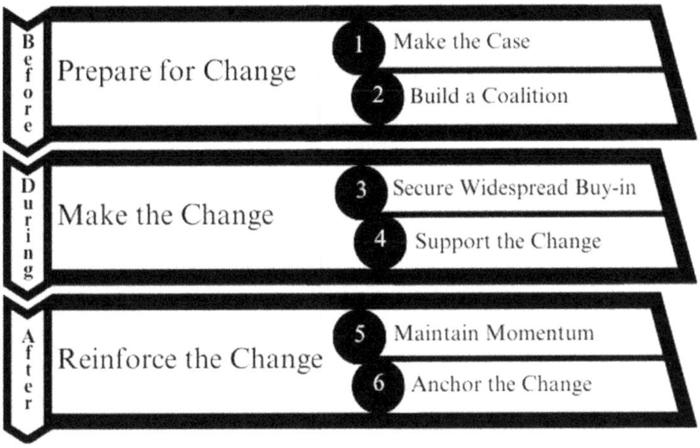

Figure 6.2 Change Phases and Steps. *Source*: Ashley Amos.

Phase 1: Prepare for Change

Step 1: Make the Case

Once a changemaker has had the lightbulb moment, their first step is to figure out how to communicate their idea to others. This involves not only articulating what the change will achieve but also why now is the time to tackle it.

Every change needs a vision of the future that makes it worth doing. Imagine where the institution will be once this change is successfully implemented. This visioning exercise can be similar to the creation of a vision in the strategic planning process. It is the end goal from which the actions needed to reach it can be derived. Developing a vision helps clarify the scope of the change. Being clear about what is changing is just as important as being clear about what is not changing.[16] A clear definition of the change will enhance understanding and provide reassurance in an uncertain time.

Once the changemaker has demonstrated why a change is needed, they must answer the question of why now. Without a sense of urgency, even those who agree that change would be beneficial may want to table it for another time.[17] The changemaker must be able to get people thinking about what the world would look like with the change in place and motivate them to move forward.

When making the case for change, the changemaker should avoid simply cheerleading the effort; generating support requires more than superficial excitement.[18] The communication developed should anticipate resistance and prepare answers to real questions likely to be raised.

Information can be a powerful tool in convincing others that a change is needed. Perhaps the change would capitalize on an opportunity, reduce a risk, or address declining financial performance. The changemaker can draw on available information from within the institution, make comparisons to other similarly situated institutions, or make predictions about which way economic, social, or political winds will blow. The changemaker must package this information to persuade others that the institution would be better off with the change than without it.

Making the case for change may be step 1, but the vision and urgency established in this step will be continually repeated and reinforced throughout the change management lifecycle. More people will become involved as the change progresses. Supporters may need to be reminded of the end goal if support wavers along the way. New information will be learned as action steps are identified and resistance is encountered that will sharpen the initial definition of change.

As we proceed through each step of the change management process, consider the example of a museum embarking on a reorganization. Imagine that a new director has joined the museum. The museum planned for this change in leadership and timed its current strategic plan to sunset one year after the new director had joined the museum. Thus, the new director spends some time observing and evaluating the museum as they begin to develop the next iteration of the strategic plan.

The new director notes that the museum has fallen behind on a number of goals and objectives in the current strategic plan. Parts of the institution that own related pieces of the work have not been working together in a concerted and efficient way to advance the museum's priorities. During a town hall with museum leaders, an office head opines that the real problem is that the organizational structure hasn't changed since the museum opened, and years of growth have led to misalignment between the museum's strategic direction and its legacy organization.

The director thinks the office head has some interesting ideas and asks them to schedule a meeting to lay them out more fully. The office head is now positioned to take on the role of change agent—and the new director as change sponsor—if they are able to make the case for change.

The office head begins to leverage available data and their own institutional knowledge to demonstrate why the current organizational structure is not serving the museum. They analyze information on strategic plan implementation to identify areas of poor performance. They draw connections between their understanding of historical development of various offices, such as how the addition of new functions or changes in leadership led them to their current state. They review financial data to show how duplicative responsibilities among siloed offices have led to wasteful spending on similar functions in different parts of the museum.

The office head pairs this information with an argument for the urgency of the change. They propose that the reorganization be designed concurrent with the strategic plan. By aligning the organizational structure with the plan's strategic goals, the museum will be better positioned to achieve them.

The office head takes all that they have prepared to the meeting with the director and makes their pitch. Having laid out a future for the museum where the entire organization is rowing in the same direction, the office head has helped the director see that the time is right to make this change.

Step 2: Build a Coalition of Support

Once the changemaker has built the case for change, it's time to deploy those arguments to enlist an initial coalition of supporters. This step is the beginning of an influencing campaign that continues throughout the change management lifecycle.

These key partners will join the changemaker as a guiding force for change. They do not necessarily need to be at the top of the leadership hierarchy—and in some cases, it may be best if they are not. These individuals should be well-positioned to contribute to or champion the change. Perhaps they represent an office that is a key player in the change. Or they are a savvy communicator who can help garner support. The people chosen for the coalition should help the changemaker access as many supporters as possible at all levels and across different stakeholder groups.

Once the changemaker has successfully made the case for change, the assembled coalition can build out a detailed action plan. Their diverse perspectives and skills will contribute to identifying the participants, resources, and timelines for implementing the change successfully.[19] The action plan should consider both the organizational and behavioral changes needed to make the change successful. Since the coalition is likely to differ from established hierarchy or governance, the action plan should be reviewed and approved by these structures as needed.

Returning to our reorganization example, the office head and director are considering who to seek out from across the museum to join their coalition. The changemakers want to include the head of strategic planning because the contents of the strategic plan will shape what the future organization will look like. Early support from human resources, building operations, and finance will be essential to transitioning personnel, funding, and physical space during the reorganization.

Perhaps the changemakers identify a museum leader who has a long history at the institution and has taken a leading role in prior modernization initiatives. This person may be a strong ally in convincing other long-time employees that the current structure no longer meets their needs. To diversify the levels of leadership in the coalition, they also target a team leader who has already successfully forged informal relationships across organizational boundaries to improve a disjointed process. This person can provide insights into challenges currently being faced at the working level.

These prospective partners are the first test of the changemakers' ability to make the case for change to a wider audience. These coalition members were chosen for a reason. Their support will enable the change management effort to benefit from their knowledge and experience. Together, they can turn the idea for change into a plan of action.

They can dig deeper into the strategic planning timeline to identify when that process will be far enough along to inform the new organizational structure. They can collect more information from coalition members to inform the desired future organizational structure. They can plan the personnel actions that would be needed to realign employees to new hierarchies and titles or make changes to job descriptions when parts of a role are changed. They outline the steps to change office names in financial and human resources systems. They map out how to update budget structures when office budgets are split or consolidated and align the timing of these changes with the budget cycle.

As the action plan comes together for the organizational elements of the change, the coalition builds out the behavioral elements in tandem. They prepare a communication strategy that ties in with strategic plan engagement to help impacted employees understand how the reorganization will support the museum's forthcoming goals. They focus on offices that will be most affected by the reorganization. They target employees who are involved in the budget formulation process, as aligning funds to the new structure is one of the early steps to make the change. They identify specific employees that will likely resist the change as well as others who may become vocal advocates if involved early. With a strong plan for both organizational and behavioral change in hand, the coalition is ready to start to make the reorganization a reality.

Phase 2: Make the Change

Step 3: Secure Widespread Support

Armed with a strong case for change and a plan to carry it out, the coalition seeks to gain the buy-in of as many impacted employees as possible. Without a broad desire for change, the change effort will not be able to gain the momentum needed to be implemented.

In this step, the coalition expands the message and communication strategies developed in phase one and adapts to directly address resistance as it is encountered. Communication should not be limited to change-focused briefings. The coalition should seek opportunities in daily work to emphasize how things would be different after the change.

Communication also must be two-way. When people are given a part to play in the change process, they have a greater sense of control in an uncertain time. A participatory environment can also help improve the action plan for change. Perhaps impacted employees identified old processes or practices that would be obstacles to the change. The coalition may realize that siloed thinking is limiting their ability to get multiple affected teams to collaborate. A change management approach that adapts to this new information is more likely to generate the momentum needed to outpace pockets of resistance.

In our reorganization example, the assembled coalition is now carrying out their communication strategy to reach employees impacted by the change. Their approach begins by sharing across the institution that a reorganization is being developed. Without defining the new structure, they can share their intent to link the organizational structure to the new strategic plan. This approach has the benefit of bringing people in early, but risks negative reactions. Rumors can quickly begin to swirl when the details of the change are unknown.

The coalition ensures their initial presentation tempers fears by providing assurances about what will not change. Employees will want to hear that no one is losing their job and no functions are being eliminated. While some people may have past experience with reorganizations that simply moved boxes on an organizational chart to no real end, this reorganization is intended to meaningfully improve the way they work together to deliver the museum's mission.

As the coalition seeks to broaden support, they will continue adjusting their strategy. Perhaps a part of the museum that will remain relatively unchanged turns out to have one of the most vocal resistors, so they increase their focus on an office they had initially discounted in favor of those facing more significant disruption of their operations. They continuously reevaluate the number of rounds of engagement needed with different stakeholder groups and make decisions about the best forums to hold and the right talking points to address the type of resistance encountered.

Perhaps the discussion in these forums provides new talking points when impacted employees identify current organizational pain points that would be improved by the new structure. The coalition can follow up with these employees to get them more involved with the change project. Employees will be more supportive as they see that their feedback is helping to design new ways of working together under the reorganization.

The process of garnering support continues as the coalition monitors progress across multiple groups of impacted employees—strong personalities, vocal resistors, key positions, and representatives of a constituency of employees—until they reach a tipping point where they feel like the institution is more ready than not to take on this change.

Step 4: Support the Change

When support has reached the tipping point, it's time to implement the change. Depending on the complexity of the change, fully implementing the change may require successive actions over weeks, months, or years. Breaking down the change into more digestible pieces makes the change seem more attainable than taking it on as one big bite. The longer the path to full implementation, the more opportunities there are to evaluate progress and ensure the change is going according to plan.

As progress reports begin to show early successes, the coalition can choose the right time to tackle the tougher aspects of the change—those that hinged on the support of a critical holdout or that may have felt overwhelming if changed earlier. This is the time to target the remaining few impacted employees who had not bought in when the change was merely theoretical. Consider swapping out early contributors who may be in need of a break with latecomers to bring fresh energy to the effort. Converts may prove to be excellent salespeople to anyone still on the fence.

Collecting employee feedback about what is working and what isn't enables adjustments along the way. Even setbacks can be reframed as progress by communicating the lesson learned and how it will make the change effort even more successful.

The coalition should leverage employee feedback to ensure that resources and support are directed to the areas of greatest need. Impacted employees may need multiple rounds of training and individualized support to ensure no one is left behind. Other employees who are quick to adapt to change should be acknowledged. Positive reinforcement boosts the morale of those who are exemplifying the change and helps demonstrate to others how this success can be replicated.

In our reorganization example, the coalition's plan of action would have scheduled an effective date for the new organizational structure. Let's say the coalition opted to schedule the reorganization on the first day of the new budget year. This date enables personnel and budget movements to occur cleanly at the start of a new year. The date also aligns with the strategic plan's effective date, allowing them to begin tracking how the strategic plan is being implemented under the new organizational structure.

While a date may have been set for the change, the reorganization does not happen overnight. Months prior, the budget formulation process established how funds and personnel will be realigned. The human resources office prepared the paperwork for personnel changes. The new office names were created in human resources and financial systems ready to be activated. On the day of the reorganization, these changes are applied in each system and communicated to offices and individual employees.

The coalition understands that the day of the change may feel abrupt for employees who are less involved in these preparatory actions. Disruption of regular ways of working may cause even supportive employees to question if this reorganization is having the intended effect.

The coalition doubles down on communication efforts. They continue to seek feedback and give platforms to employees who have ideas about how to improve how the new structure operates. They assemble working groups focused on addressing obstacles that have arisen during the transition, such as misaligned workflows and processes. They provide training and support to employees who have not effectively integrated into the new organizational structure. Together, these efforts help the coalition not only maintain support, but expand it to include previous resistors who begin to see how the new organization can work for them.

Phase 3: Reinforce the Change

Step 5: Maintain Momentum

After the change is implemented, formal change management structures may start winding down from their peak levels. The actions needed to carry out the change have been checked off the list and those shepherding the change need to return to their regular duties. The pressure to reach the finish line has subsided and people are feeling the effects of change fatigue. Daily responsibilities move back to the forefront.

Successful change implementation should not give a false sense of accomplishment. The change effort must be prevented from stalling out when the act of making the change is no longer the central focus. Day-to-day operations will provide opportunities to either apply the change to a new circumstance or regress to old ways of doing business.

Repetition helps impacted employees build the muscle memory needed to change habits no matter what scenario they face in their work. Repeated application of the change also demonstrates that the change is working in practice. Scenarios where the change is not a perfect fit help identify where further tweaks are needed to optimize the change.

Each new application of the change contributes to the message. But it is their cumulative power that generates momentum toward success on larger and larger scales. Constant communication tying the wins back to the vision for change reinforces that the imagined future is becoming a reality.

Returning to our reorganization example, the coalition stays in contact with supporters across the museum. They learn of examples where new ways of working have opened doors. At a museum-wide staff meeting, they invite two teams to share how they have successfully combined their related initiatives for greater impact. As strategic plan implementation begins to show results, they highlight how the new organizational structure facilitated progress, tying back to the reorganization's vision of creating an institution better aligned to its strategic goals.

The first budget formulation process after the reorganization provides another opportunity to reinforce the change. Unlike the last budget formulation that moved personnel and resources to match a reorganization that was not yet a reality, this time budget owners have experience in the new structure to inform their budget decisions. They may find more efficiencies and ways to align work that the museum can spotlight as further evidence that operations are changing as intended.

Step 6: Anchor the Change

With the benefits of reinforcement under its belt, the institution can take the final step to lock in the change through institutional culture. At any time after a change, the change agent may move into a new role, the change sponsor may retire, and impacted employees may depart. Unexpected events may tempt the institution to abandon the change and return to familiar old ways. The change needs to be so embedded in the institution that the first response is to apply or adapt the change to the new reality rather than throw it out the window.

As the change management team is winding down, they should transfer permanent ownership to someone who will be responsible for sustaining the new steady state. Most importantly, the change must be encapsulated in the institution's values. Themes from the original vision about why the change is so needed and how it will bring the institution into the future can be echoed through value statements, strategic planning priorities, and employee engagement.

Depending on the nature of the change and the stability of the institution, the third phase of change management may need to continue long after the change is made. This should not be surprising, nor should it be discouraging. Persistent effort to reinforce the change will ensure the institution is able to grow and evolve its culture in alignment with its values.

In our reorganization example, the museum has settled into the change, and it's time for the change management team to return to their regular work. Before they do, they ensure all the lessons from the implementation have been documented. Documentation include changes to job descriptions, policies and procedures, training modules, and new employee orientation materials.

The changemakers have already positioned the change to become part of the culture and values of the institution by building it in alignment with the strategic plan. As strategic plan implementation is ongoing, the results of the reorganization will continue to imbed into museum culture. The head of strategic planning may be the right person to assign ongoing ownership of the reorganization. They are well positioned to monitor how effectively the structure continues to support the strategic plan, and they can include reevaluation of the structure when the next strategic plan is under development. This continuity will help meet the original vision of ensuring the organizational structure never again diverges from the museum's strategic direction.

Years after the reorganization, perhaps the museum faces an unexpected financial downturn. The museum will undergo a new round of change in response to its changing environment. As the director helps the institution navigate this change, they may find opportunities to credit the reorganization with helping to put the museum in a position to adapt to these new circumstances. Years of effort to identify financial efficiencies and build connections between previously siloed programs have prepared the institution and the workforce for the next challenge on the horizon. In making these connections, the director both cements the vision of the reorganization as an institutional value and encourages employees as they embark on a new period of change.

FIRM CONNECTIONS

Change is never easy, and it requires a significant amount of time, effort, and people to accomplish. Change management is part of FIRM's Integration pillar because it enables an institution to undertake concerted, large-scale actions to improve its financial health and stability. Together with governance, change management should be embedded into implementation of other FIRM building blocks to ensure their integration into museum culture and operations.

The value of strong governance and change management has already been discussed in the budgeting and strategic planning chapters. However, the benefits of change management are not limited to the Integration side of FIRM. The Resilience pillar involves asking an institution to change the way it thinks about and addresses future uncertainty. How these building blocks are communicated, carried out, and collaborated on across an institution will have a significant impact on the long-term success of FIRM.

Part IV

THE RESILIENCE PILLAR

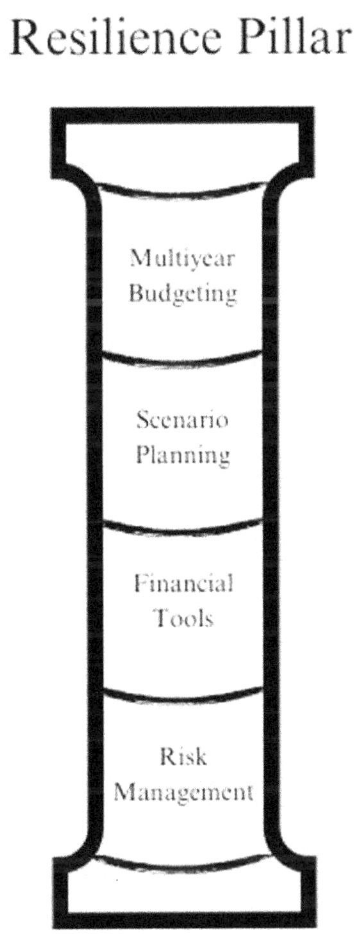

Chapter 7

Risk Management

RESILIENCE BUILDING BLOCK 1

Risk management is the first building block of FIRM's Resilience pillar. Just as a strong strategy-to-budget connection underpins an institution's ability to advance as a cohesive unit, active management of risks enables an institution to anticipate the obstacles it may encounter along its path. Consideration of risk prevents a museum from only planning for the way it *wants* the world to be, causing plans to be derailed while it reacts to changes in its environment after they have occurred. This chapter will explore how to build the capacity for identifying, managing, and monitoring risks by ensuring risk is incorporated into the budgeting and strategic planning processes.

Risk is the potential for loss, harm, or negative consequences that may occur when undertaking a particular action. Risk management involves deciding how best to address the potential future problem and the associated outcome. Many of the consequences commonly associated with risk are financial in nature. The risk of losing money incentivizes advanced planning and action to reduce or otherwise protect against the potential loss.

Since the fourteenth century, arrangements with investors enabled mariners to shift the risks associated with lost ships or cargo to others, preventing events like piracy, hurricanes, or shipwrecks from being ruinous.[1] By the seventeenth century, the Lloyd's coffee house became a hub for brokers to share shipping information and write policies for upcoming voyages.[2] Today, Lloyd's of London has evolved into an international insurance company.[3] A museum that reduces its internal risks by anticipating a potential problem and then providing for a solution will be a more resilient institution when future problems arise and will be more likely to weather a storm.

In 1752, Benjamin Franklin helped found the Philadelphia Contributionship for the Insurance of Houses from Loss by Fire to address the dangerous conditions within the densely populated community of wood-framed houses.[4] Policyholders paid for insurance and were required to implement safety measures like lightning rods and chimney inspections.[5] The Contributionship conducted inspections to evaluate the fire risk associated with each property.[6] This approach not only protected individual policyholders but created a sense of collective action among policyholders working toward a shared goal. There are several lessons that a museum can learn from this example, including the importance of defining and understanding its risks and the application of various strategies to take action against these risks.

Risky financial behaviors such as excessive stock speculation, lack of bank regulations, and excessive borrowing contributed to the American stock market crash of 1929.[7] In the aftermath of this catastrophic event, the U.S. Congress passed legislation like the Securities Act of 1933 and the Glass–Steagall Act.[8] Legislation and regulations for investors, stock brokers, and banks to prevent excessive speculation and conflicts of interest were effectively a risk management strategy for the U.S. economy.[9] As the government did in this example, museums may need to act on multiple fronts to address various forms of risky behavior. A museum that identifies related risks can avoid having to respond to multiple failures across its financial ecosystem.

In each of these historical examples, risk management was a response to a problem that already occurred. A merchant's ship was plundered, a house fire turned an entire block to ash, and a financial crisis wreaked havoc on the economy. Perhaps the incident happened to someone else, raising fear in others who were similarly situated that they may suffer the same fate one day. Regardless, the mishap brought attention to an existing risk, along with a realization that the next incident could be even worse. True risk management requires an anticipatory rather than reactive posture. The resilient institution does not wait for the worst to happen and then scramble to make changes in its wake.

IDENTIFYING RISKS

Risk management begins from the bottom up. An individual office may consider what are those things that may keep the office from accomplishing its goals. The process of identifying risks and building connections between them can vary widely in terms of difficulty. Some risks will be top of mind for museum leaders based on their day-to-day responsibilities.

The information technology (IT) office may easily identify the risk associated with having outdated desktop computers deployed across the museum. The human resources director may already be concerned about the lack of succession planning for key personnel reaching retirement age when asked to identify their risks. A program head may have started raising questions about the physical space and environmental controls needed for safe archival storage. These potential events are known to the museum and need only be translated into the language and structure of risk management.

Other risks can be identified by thinking about more significant potential events outside of daily work. Institutions are focusing on known risks and probabilities and may not consider outlier events. A museum may need to think about what it would do in the event of the sudden loss or theft of irreplaceable artifacts. Consider the potential that the museum falls victim to an insider threat. In 2016, Wells Fargo bank paid over $3 billion to settle criminal and civil lawsuits after employees and managers engaged in a scheme to pad their sales figures by opening millions of unauthorized customer bank accounts.[10] A museum employee and their partners could misuse information or system privileges to compromise sensitive donor data or siphon off museum funds. No museum, no matter how successful, should fail to consider a plan that would limit the risk associated with bad actors within their own environment. Limiting a risk register or risk discussion to only events that have happened to your museum would significantly limit the importance of learning from risk events that have happened in other disciplines and hamper your institution's ability to plan for future risk events.

The so-called black swan events are even more improbable but bring about catastrophic results.[11] In 2010, the Deepwater Horizon oil rig explosion changed the way we think about the havoc that can be wreaked by an oil spill.[12] Eleven lives were lost and four million barrels of oil spilled into the Gulf of Mexico over 87 days, making the event the largest oil spill in marine drilling history.[13] Prior to COVID-19, it is unlikely that many museums listed a global pandemic among their risks. Being prepared for the worst possible event highlights the importance of resilience and integration within the institution.

A robust brainstorming exercise may not be able to predict these exact events as potential risks, but thorough examination of risk may lead to scenarios that share some features. Perhaps a museum has plans for how to manage some level of public health event, which could be a starting point if a much more significant event occurs. Any plan is better than no plan at all. The more rigor an institution applies to the interrogation of risk, the more likely it is to be resilient in the face of any future event.[14]

FIRM CONNECTIONS: GOVERNANCE AND CHANGE MANAGEMENT

Risk management can be carried out by an individual office head seeking to improve their risk posture or as an institution-wide process. Consider the example of a museum's visitor services team wanting to plan for potential problems during the busy season. The team identifies the actions that should be taken in advance to ensure orderly access by a large number of visitors. Visitor services could stop there—planning only for the risks that directly affect its work—or it could broaden the risk management effort by comparing risks with other offices. Physical security and concessions teams may have their own concerns about the busy season and may find commonalities or gaps in their conception of their risks.

As risk management elevates to the institutional level, the museum director may be concerned about maintaining the museum's reputation of accessibility. Building an integrated understanding of risks across the institution allows the museum to better determine the appropriate actions to take at each organizational level.

The involvement of offices across the museum and consideration of risk at multiple organizational levels requires strong connections between the resilience and integration pillars of FIRM. Connections to the strategic planning and budgeting building blocks will be discussed later in this chapter, but two integration principles key to establishing risk management within an institution are governance and change management.

A museum that is just starting its risk management journey may already informally consider risk as a discussion point when making strategic and financial decisions. Perhaps museum leaders are making decisions as a reaction to an emergent situation or based on reflections on past events that ended poorly. Temporary or ad hoc groups may be convened to address specific problems, but the museum is not systematically collecting risk information and proactively tracking risk-related data. The museum lacks a strategy for long-term, institution-wide risk management.

Proactive risk management must be part of the museum's culture to ensure that it is better prepared to navigate uncertainties and challenges. Museums have committees and boards for a variety of important priorities, such as education, outreach, finance, and scholarship; effective risk management requires the same level of institutional commitment.

In larger organizations, the specific position of Chief Risk Officer (CRO) may be created to institutionalize risk management and facilitate the governance structure. A museum may not necessarily need a full-time CRO, but it certainly needs an employee or board member that leads the risk management process for the institution. The CRO sets a cadence for regular dialogue and monitoring within an established governance structure.

Governance provides a forum for taking practical and detailed steps to ensure the institution can withstand events that may threaten its short- and long-term stability. The governance structure should consist of multiple levels of leaders looking at the museum through different lenses. Office heads need to identify, track, and monitor the risks in their respective areas. This information would then flow across to other offices who may identify similar risks or interdependencies. The information also flows up to an executive leadership group responsible for overseeing office-level progress and identifying common risks that require elevation to a multi-office or institutional level. The museum director and the museum's board will carry out a similar function for those risks that are elevated to the institutional level.

While most staff of the museum will not be directly participating in the governance structure, their engagement is essential for successful integration of risk management into the culture of the museum. Office heads must communicate their risk management priorities and strategies to their employees and ensure staff understand how the actions they take may impact risk. If risk identification and monitoring is meant to start from the bottom up, employees are on the front line of risk management.

BUILDING A RISK REGISTER

The CRO must establish a means to systematically track risks and the efforts to impact those risks across multiple offices and levels of the institution. A risk register is a risk monitoring template that serves as the central repository for essential details related to risks. A risk register template can take the form of a simple document or software tool, depending on the level of sophistication a museum applies to risk management. Use of a template can be a valuable tool to support the institutionalization of risk management by providing a shared language and standardized format to guide risk discussions. Not all templates are the same, but a risk register will generally include the following key pieces of information: risk description, risk owner, risk category, priority, risk management strategy, and key risk indicators.

Risk Description

An accurate description of the risk is an important first step in establishing the scope of all other fields of the risk register. Risk descriptions should be framed as "if/then" statements. Throughout this section, we will return to our example of a museum with an outdated visitor ticketing system to illustrate how the fields of the risk register are populated. Visitor services

Table 7.1 Elements of a Risk Register

Elements of a risk register	
Definition	If the risk event or condition occurs, then what is the potential consequence?
Owner	Who is accountable for managing the risk?
Category	What type(s) of consequence are of concern?
Priority	What is the likelihood and impact?
Strategy	What is the approach to managing the risk?
KRIs	How will the risk be measured and monitored?

Source: Ashley Amos.

would describe the risk as follows: if there is a visitor ticketing system outage, then visitors will not be able to schedule their visit to the museum and will not have access to the collection.

Risk Owner

The risk owner is accountable for managing the risk described in the risk register. Assigning risk owners helps improve accountability and enhances the effectiveness of risk management efforts. It is important that the risk owner be a specific individual rather than an office. In our ticketing system example, it is not enough to name the visitor services office as the risk owner; the appropriate risk owner is the director of visitor services.

Risk Category

As the list of risk descriptions begins to take shape, each should be assigned a risk category. Risk categories allow for grouping of risks based on their potential consequences. Risk categories can include operational, financial, legal, or reputational risks, among others.

The visitor ticketing system example described above would be an operational risk because the concern of the visitor services team relates to visitor experience and accessibility.

A financial risk may be if a museum's endowment suffers sustained market losses, then the payouts will no longer be sufficient to support the budget.

A legal risk may be if a museum violates donor intent on a restricted gift by using funds for expenses outside of the specified purpose, then the donor may make a claim that the museum violated the terms and conditions of the grant agreement.

A reputational risk may be if a large corporate or individual donor is accused of a misdeed, then the museum could be subject to unwanted negative publicity and face public pressure to distance itself from the donor.

Each category represents an aspect of potential harm resulting from a risk event. Organizing risks into categories can help a risk owner better articulate the root of their concern. This exercise can refine the risk description and more clearly point toward what actions are needed

Figure 7.1 Risk Categories. *Source*: Ashley Amos.

to address it. Categorization can be especially important when a risk has multiple facets. Many risks will not neatly fit into only one category.

Consider how to categorize our example of the outdated visitor ticketing system. Visitor services may view this as a reputational risk: visitors' experience with the museum may be negatively impacted if the system goes down when they are completing their online booking. The program office managing the collection may view this as an operational risk: a system outage may limit accessibility of the collection. IT may see a different facet of operational risk: an outdated system may have vulnerabilities that create a weak point in the museum's cybersecurity posture. The finance office may see it as a financial risk: lost revenue from a long-term outage may have a budget impact if the museum relies on entrance fees.

Each of these offices is correct in its assessment of the risk. A risk register can help organize and integrate these various concerns. Each office should include their articulation of the risk under their ownership in the risk register. Perhaps all offices included this ticketing system risk in their first attempt at filling out the risk register. Perhaps when assembled in the risk management governance structure, some offices heard the ticketing system raised by others and realized they too shared an aspect of this risk and should add it to their risk register.

Now that the risk has been fully captured through the lens of each stakeholder, the CRO can leverage the governance structure to elevate the suite of risks to executive leadership. Executive leadership determines how to articulate the consolidated risk at the institutional level. Perhaps they determine that they are most concerned about the operational risks: access to the collection and cybersecurity vulnerability. They can categorize the institutional-level risk as operational and focus the monitoring at their level of governance on the action steps that mitigate the operational concerns.

Risk Priority

Not every risk is equal. Institutions cannot and should not try to address every potential risk regardless of its size. But how can an institution compare a myriad of seemingly unrelated risks and choose which to focus on? A risk register can facilitate prioritization of identified risks by assigning a priority score. The priority is derived from a combined view of two scaling factors: impact and likelihood.

Impact refers to the consequences the museum will face if the risk event occurs. Likelihood refers to the probability that a risk event will occur. Both impact and likelihood are considered on a scale from low to high. A high-impact event has substantial and widespread consequences, leading to major disruptions or lasting changes on a large scale. A high-likelihood event is predicted with a significant prospect of being realized in the absence of intervention. These factors may point in different directions for the same risk: an event can be highly probable but have a relatively small consequence, or inversely, devastating consequences but not considered likely to occur.

The risk register may assign a scale of numerical (e.g., 1–5) or descriptive (e.g., low, medium, and high) ratings to help risk owners assess each factor. Once each risk has been scaled for both likelihood and impact, the results can be plotted on a quad chart, with each quadrant representing one of four potential combinations of the two factors: low impact/low likelihood, high impact/low likelihood, low impact/high likelihood, and high impact/high likelihood. The risk owner places a data point on the quad chart to reflect the rating of each risk across the vertical and horizontal axes.

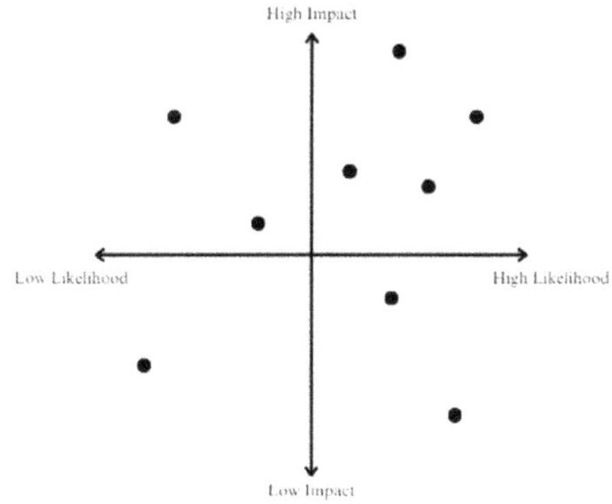

Figure 7.2 Quad Chart Populated with Risks. *Source*: Ashley Amos.

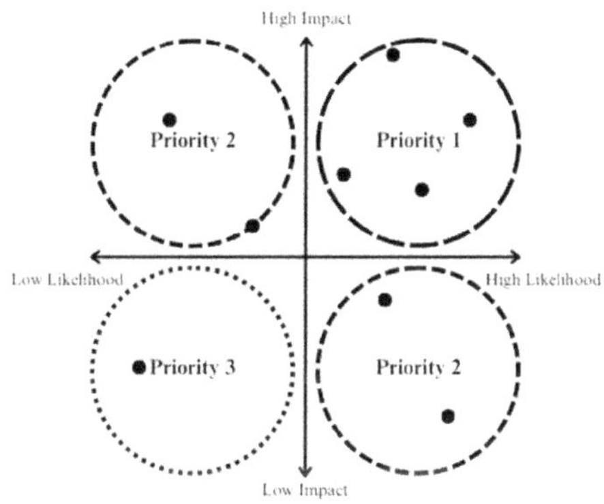

Figure 7.3 Prioritization of Risks in Each Quadrant. *Source*: Ashley Amos.

Assembling all risks on the quad chart begins to reveal the relative priority of otherwise unconnected risks. Points in the top right quadrant (high impact/high likelihood) pose the greatest threat to the institution and should be the primary area of focus for risk management activities. Points in the bottom left quadrant (low impact/low likelihood) are relatively modest threats and may not be deemed worthy of devoting much effort to address them. The two remaining quadrants, which have a mix of high and low ratings, together comprise the middle tier of risk priorities. These risks should be addressed to the extent that time and financial resources allow. The priority level (1–3) assigned to each risk should be included in a field in the risk register alongside the other details about the particular risk.

In our visitor ticketing system example, the director of visitor services assesses both the likelihood and impact of the operational risk based on the information available. A system outage may be relatively unlikely if the system is only just reaching the end of its lifecycle, but may be judged to have a high impact if an entire day's visitors have to be turned away or ticketed by hand or in cash. The director places the data point representing this risk in the high-impact/low-likelihood quadrant of the chart. The risk is therefore considered priority level two. The director should devote less resources to this risk than those in the priority one quadrant and carefully balance how to handle this risk compared to others at the priority two level.

Risk Management Strategy

All the information collected about a risk is building toward the most important part of the risk register: the development and execution of a risk management strategy. A risk management strategy requires making a decision about what, if anything, the risk owner will do about the identified risk. Risk management can be grouped into four primary strategies: avoidance, acceptance, transfer, and reduction. The selection of a particular strategy guides the risk owner toward the appropriate actions needed to carry out that strategy.

Risk avoidance involves removal of the risk by sidestepping it altogether. In our ticketing system example, the risk owner could implement an avoidance strategy by divesting from the technology and requiring that tickets be purchased in-person at the museum.

Risk acceptance means the risk owner has made the decision to face the danger head on. In our ticketing system example, an acceptance strategy would not take any actions to reduce the likelihood of an outage. Perhaps the visitor services team simply places a warning banner on the museum website, stating that tickets can be purchased onsite if the online ticketing system is unavailable.

Risk transfer refers to the process of shifting the consequences of a risk from one party to another. This is most common in a museum acquiring an insurance policy, extended warranties, or incorporating white glove service into a contract. In the ticketing system example, the museum may go back to the ticketing system vendor to make changes to the contract to add technical support. Paying for the additional support services effectively shifts the responsibility for operating the outdated system from the museum to the vendor.

Risk reduction is a set of actions designed to lessen the impact or likelihood that the risk will occur, thus helping the risk move down to a lower-priority level. The goal is to increase resiliency against known risks by mitigating their adverse effects or potential occurrence. In our ticketing system example, actions under a risk reduction strategy could include working with IT on an outage recovery plan to reduce downtime, training visitor services staff on contingency procedures to allow visitor access during a system outage, and making plans for the acquisition of a new system that is more reliable.

The risk management strategy selected by the risk owner may be influenced by a number of considerations. A low-priority risk may be more acceptable because it is not expected to cause much damage if it occurs at all; tolerating this risk allows more attention to be focused on higher risk priorities. The risk category may also shape the chosen course of action: perhaps

Figure 7.4 Risk Management Strategies. *Source*: Ashley Amos.

risk management governance chooses to devote extra attention to operational risks. The realities of resource availability are likely to put the most pressure on selection of a strategy. In our ticketing system example, the risk reduction strategy of purchasing a new system would not be possible without the funds to support it.

Key Risk Indicators

Risk management is not a static process. The nature of a risk may have changed since it was originally described and prioritized. Progress on risk reduction actions may have stalled, failing to mitigate risk as intended. The need for continuous risk monitoring is as important as the identification of the risk itself.

Key risk indicators (KRIs) provide a data-driven methodology to measure risk. Risk management governance may choose to review KRIs monthly or quarterly to look for changes over time. KRIs serve two important functions. First, they associate data points with a risk, allowing multiple comparison points that help reveal how a risk may be changing. Second, they can provide a warning signal when a risk is on the path to becoming a reality.

If we carry the example of an outdated visitor ticketing system through the KRI process, the risk owner can develop quantifiable ways to measure this risk. The first KRI could measure the average time it takes a visitor to complete their ticket purchase in the system. Perhaps the system is stalling or freezing mid-purchase or not retaining visitor selections when clicking through multiple screens. This data may already be available within system metrics, or visitor services may need to work with the system vendor to establish such metrics.

If the data is available, visitor services may want to go a step further, breaking out the online purchases from the in-person purchases from a visitor services employee or an automated kiosk. The risk owner can monitor the average time it takes to complete purchases through various means to understand the extent to which staff member support, either directly at the ticketing desk or by assisting at a kiosk, is mitigating some of the system malfunctions. While the KRI will not define these specific causes, the elevated time to purchase will indicate that system malfunctions are becoming more frequent and additional investigation is needed to address these malfunctions.

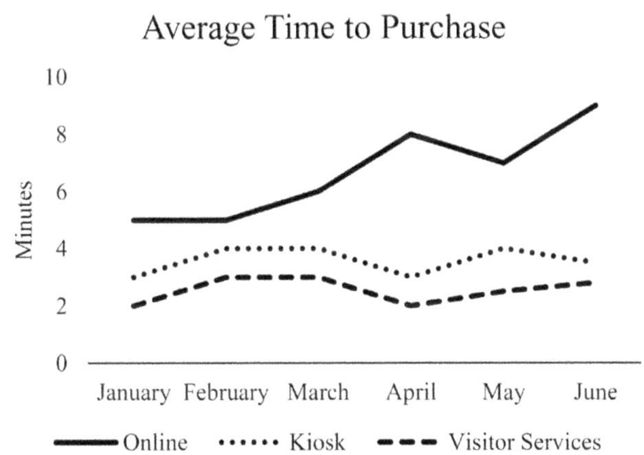

Figure 7.5 Key Risk Indicator Measuring Average Time to Purchase a Ticket Using Various Methods. *Source*: Ashley Amos.

The first KRI tracks the time to complete a ticket purchase, but the risk owner may also want to track how many ticket purchases were initiated but never completed. Perhaps the system kicked out the user and required multiple attempts before a successful purchase or a visitor abandoned their incomplete order in frustration. This second KRI can measure the percentage of total system traffic that resulted in incomplete versus complete orders. As this KRI is monitored, an increase in the percent of orders that are incomplete will indicate that system malfunctions are hindering visitors from gaining access to the museum.

Not all risks have readily available quantitative data that can help a risk owner build KRIs. The risk owner can try to convert qualitative information into measurable and repeatable data. Perhaps the ticketing system does not provide the usage metrics that enable the tracking of the two KRIs described above, or the risk owner wants to measure more about the visitor experience in the system that cannot be discerned from this data. The risk owner may add a survey to the end of each ticket order that asks users to rate their experience.

Surveys are a common way to convey qualitative information such as satisfaction or enjoyment as quantifiable data using a numerical or descriptive scale (e.g., a rating of 1–5 or a choice of terms like very satisfied, neutral, or not satisfied). Not all users will complete a survey, but tracking the responses received over time will indicate whether there has been a change in the functionality of the ticketing system that is affecting visitor experience.

These KRIs are unique to visitor services' ticketing system risk, but as we know, other museum offices are tracking related risks through their own lenses. The same underlying metrics may be valuable to other risk owners in defining their KRIs. For example, the finance office is tracking the ticket system as a financial risk due to its potential impact on budgeted revenue. The finance risk owner may use the same data about incomplete orders to estimate lost revenue. It may be possible to filter the incomplete orders by unique device identifiers to differentiate between users that were eventually successful after multiple attempts and users that gave up before completing their purchase. Finance can translate the abandoned orders into cost per ticket to estimate the amount of lost revenue. As the risk owner monitors this KRI, they can assess whether lost revenue is reaching a value that is critical to the museum budget.

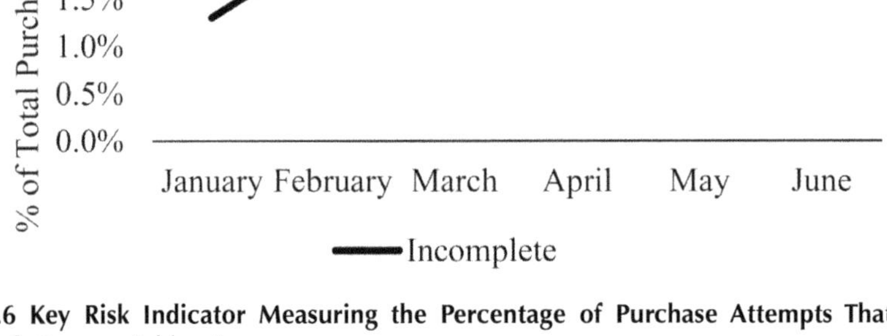

Figure 7.6 Key Risk Indicator Measuring the Percentage of Purchase Attempts That Are Not Completed. *Source*: Ashley Amos.

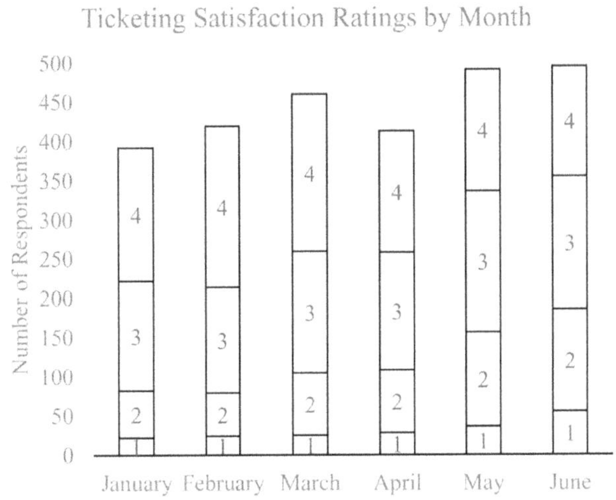

Figure 7.7 Key Risk Indicator Quantifying Visitor Satisfaction with the Ticketing Experience. *Source*: Ashley Amos.

Figure 7.8 Key Risk Indicator Measuring Lost Revenue from Abandoned Ticketing Transactions. *Source*: Ashley Amos.

The CRO will then work with the risk owners of each risk related to the ticketing system to determine which KRIs will flow up to the institutional version of this risk. Perhaps the CRO selects one KRI from each office-level risk to monitor the risk from different perspectives. Alternatively, the CRO could combine or elevate KRI metrics from different offices into a single view. Looking at our ticketing system example at the institutional level, the CRO may combine the financial and operational views of abandoned ticket purchases within one KRI to show how these events indicate growing risk from multiple perspectives.

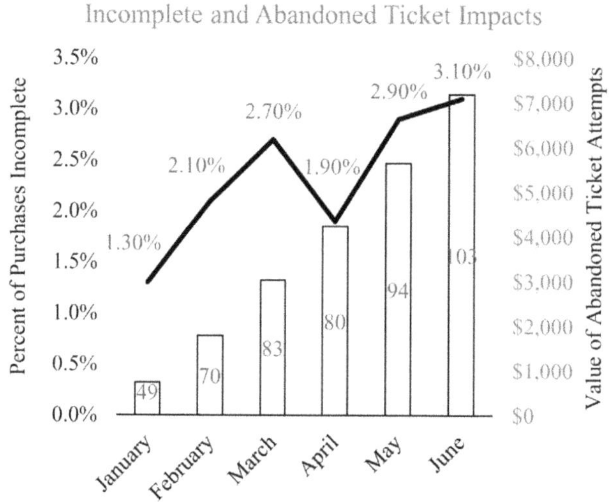

Figure 7.9 Institutional Key Risk Indicator That Provides a Consolidated View of the Number of Failed Ticket Purchases, the Percentage of Total Transactions That Are Incomplete, and the Lost Revenue from Abandoned Purchases. *Source*: Ashley Amos.

FIRM CONNECTIONS: STRATEGY AND BUDGET

We have already discussed how the establishment of risk management within an institution relies on the integration building blocks of governance and change management. As risk management becomes operational, it is critical to the integration building blocks that drive institutional direction: strategic planning and budgeting.

The articulation of risk begins with a narrow lens at the office level and broadens as risks are elevated to the institutional level. Risk management's path from office to institution is the inverse of a strategic plan, which begins with top-level strategic goals and cascades to more detailed implementation plans carried out by individual offices. These two processes can be viewed as two sides of the same coin: strategic planning defines my goals and risk management defines what might get in the way of my goals. I'll have a greater chance of succeeding if I link them together.

Strategic planning and risk management will also have natural linkages because they both require governance at multiple levels of the institution. Membership of each governance structure will likely overlap or may even be identical, but the groups assemble for different purposes and with different agendas. The different perspectives of each exercise may leave blind spots unless a museum intentionally establishes linkages between the two.

Harmonizing strategic planning and risk management involves continually reevaluating one against the other. The institutional-level strategic goals may only change every 5–10 years when the strategic plan is updated. Creation or revision of a strategic plan is a critical time to evaluate whether this new strategic direction changes the nature of the risks currently being tracked. The risk should take into account not just the impact to current operations, but how the risk could get in the way of achieving the desired future state.

Returning to our visitor ticketing system example, perhaps the new strategic plan sets a goal of expanding visitor access to the museum, beneath which sits the objective of doubling visitorship. This information should change the museum's understanding of the risk. The prospect of doubling access raises the stakes for having efficient ticketing operations. Dramatic growth in system usage may increase both the likelihood and consequences of a potential outage and cause the risk to elevate from priority two to priority one. With the risk now at a higher priority level, the museum may choose a different risk management strategy than it had under its previous conception of the risk.

After initial changes are made to bring strategy and risk into alignment, these connections must be maintained throughout each process. Implementation plans detailing the actions taken toward strategic goals are living documents. A risk register similarly monitors progress toward risk management strategies. Implementation plans and risk registers should be complementary in both their actions and the timelines for those actions. Building a risk management strategy that complements the actions being taken in pursuit of the strategic goal provides an additional layer of assurance for the museum's long-term success.

The integration of strategy and risk management can only be effective if the specified actions actually occur. We have already discussed how the activities funded in the annual budget should be stepping stones toward the strategic plan's long-term goals. Similarly, a museum must align its risk management strategies with each budget cycle.

Budgeting is the way institutions decide how to allocate their resources—not just money but also time. Management of high-priority risks requires both. An office cannot assume that they can continue a full slate of projects while also taking on actions spelled out in its risk register. Part of change management is helping offices understand how to prioritize and set realistic expectations about what can be accomplished. An office may need to slow work on another project to refocus resources on actions related to a risk mitigation strategy. The office may need to request more funds to carry out those actions or engage additional contract support to increase its capacity.

Returning to our ticketing system example, let's assume that our risk owner—the director of visitor services—is also the budget owner for the visitor services office. Through their risk register, the director has selected risk reduction as the preferred risk management strategy for the outdated system. The action with the most significant mitigation impact is the acquisition of a new, more reliable system. The decision to pursue this mitigation approach must be

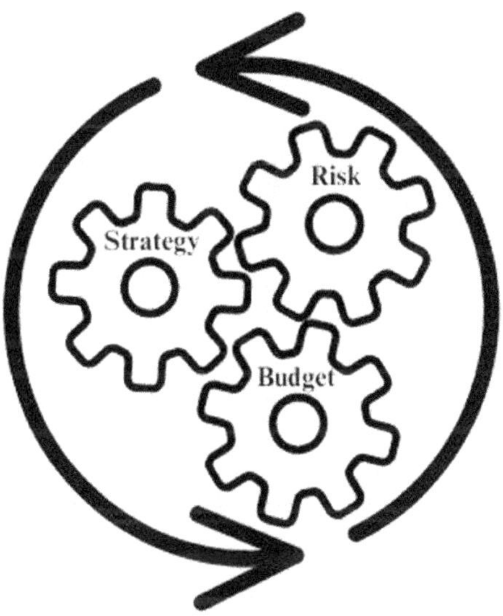

Figure 7.10 Risk, Strategy, and Budget Connections. *Source*: Ashley Amos.

carried through to budgeting. If a new system is not included in the upcoming budget, the museum will have effectively defaulted to accepting the risk for at least another year.

If the director fails in their attempt to add the new system cost to the budget, they can go back to the drawing board on which other risk management strategy to pursue. Perhaps they pivot to a risk transfer strategy that requires less funds: adding technical support from the existing system vendor.

If the risk transfer strategy still can't fit into the budget, the director may consider the risk reduction strategy of training visitor services staff to provide more hands-on ticketing support at the museum. They do not need additional funding to carry out this action, but will need to communicate through their budget that other projects or activities carried out by these staff will slow or stop for as long as staff have to continue propping up the outdated ticketing system. By actively tying risk management to the budget process, the director can lay out the options for budget governance members and help them understand how funding decisions impact risk.

FIRM CONNECTIONS

Risk management is the first building block of the Resilience pillar because many institutions naturally consider risk as they pursue their mission, but may not have harnessed the language and structures of risk management to formalize and institutionalize this way of thinking. Failure to account for risk can have significant consequences that affect the museum's financial stability. Like strategic planning, risk management is not directly a financial activity but it will only be successful if incorporated into a museum's financial ecosystem. The ability to articulate and plan for future risk expands an institution's capability for other types of resilient thinking. Risk management becomes a jumping off point for the other building blocks of the Resilience pillar: scenario planning, multi-year budgeting, and financial tools.

Chapter 8

Financial Tools

RESILIENCE BUILDING BLOCK 2

The next building block of the Resilience pillar involves the adoption of financial tools. Financial tools enhance a museum's ability to analyze historical data, understand trends, and anticipate changes to its environment. These tools allow for rapid monitoring and assessment of the museum's financial health without consuming staff time. This chapter explores how financial tools can be used by the finance office to make the entire institution more resilient. These tools can empower users throughout the museum by putting information at their fingertips and adapting to help advance financial literacy. The proactive posture fostered by financial tools reaps benefits across the building blocks of FIRM: from monitoring budget and risk to projecting future year conditions.

As the financial landscape becomes increasingly complex and dynamic, tools that help a museum navigate this uncertain terrain are more important than ever. A financial tool may be any software, instrument, or strategy used to manage and analyze financial information. These tools can range from simple spreadsheets for budgeting to complex software systems for investment analysis.

Financial tools are a resilience building block within FIRM because they can provide financial indicators that help a museum understand ongoing or potential changes to its financial circumstances. Museum leaders can actively monitor financial indicators for early warning before problems snowball. Leaders can reference these indicators as they make decisions about the museum's future direction, perhaps deciding to change their approach in light of the information that is presented.

FINANCIAL TOOL CAPABILITIES

Financial tools help institutions monitor their internal and external environment in real time through five key capabilities: accessibility, logic, connectivity, reporting, and visualization.

Figure 8.1 Capabilities of Financial Tools. *Source*: Ashley Amos.

Accessibility

Too often, employees maintain important information in documents and spreadsheets saved to their computers or perhaps a shared network or cloud-based drive accessible to other members of their team. They may have designed a spreadsheet to meet their own needs or use a template that is distributed across the institution. These files require significant manual effort to produce and maintain. They must be shared with others via email or invitation to the shared workspace, after which maintaining a definitive version may prove elusive.

Users are likely drawn to this method of capturing information not because they like to make their work more complicated, but because they don't have access to the tools they need to interact with the information in an easier way. Worse still, the tools may exist at their institution but the user does not understand how the tools can be leveraged to meet their needs.

Within these individualized uses there may be commonalities across different work groups as well as best practices that could be universally adopted. The simplest benefit to be gained from the use of a financial tool is the centralization and standardization of data. By building tools that address common use cases, all users can share and maintain information that was previously disparate. Tools that provide mere accessibility can be uncomplicated, simply asking users to manually enter data (as they would have in their personal spreadsheets) into a shared platform. Once an accessible tool has been in place for a few years, it has organically become a source of historical data that can be valuable for users interested in long-term trends.

Consider a museum that uses a risk register template for its risk management process. With the adoption of a risk tool, templates no longer need to be distributed, collected, and consolidated by the museum's CRO. Risk owners can populate fields in the software with the risk description, potential impact and likelihood, and risk management strategy. Members of the risk owner's team are also given access to the tool to update key risk indicators using the latest financial or other quantitative or qualitative data. The risk governance body can monitor changes in real time, without waiting for the CRO to consolidate template submissions and present them at the next meeting. This accessible tool allows parties at multiple levels and across the museum to maintain a shared workspace for risk management activities.

Logic

An accessible tool that relies on manual data entry can be labor intensive and carries the potential for human error. The addition of logic enables a tool to be programmed to perform certain actions with the information input by users. It can also be programmed to perform checks that improve data quality and completeness.

Let's suppose a museum adopts a tool that projects payroll costs over a ten-year span. The tool can be programmed with assumptions such as pay inflation, benefits costs, and the expected rate of employee turnover. The museum then only needs to enter its employees' current pay, apply the logic, and observe how payroll costs are projected to escalate over the ten-year period. If the projected growth appears too steep, the assumptions can be adjusted to project a more sustainable path without the need for manual recalculations.

Perhaps this museum has both union and nonunion employees with different pay scales that further complicate its projection. The museum can incorporate these pay scales in the system and build logic to assume salary increases for the applicable positions. When the pay scales change down the road, the updated versions can be added to the tool with minimal effort. The use of logic enables the museum to more easily manipulate its data and project the impacts of these changes years into the future.

Connectivity

The next level of benefits can be gained by connecting a tool to other systems and tools. Manual data entry isn't needed if a tool can be programmed to communicate with available data sources. Ideally, this connection is achieved through a direct interface so real-time changes are shared. This may not be possible if the tool is not compatible with the other system, though lesser connection types may still allow for options like a nightly data pull or manual data export and upload. The ability to integrate with existing related systems and tools is an important consideration when selecting a tool.

Let's return to our payroll projection example. While the tool uses logic to calculate anticipated cost increases, the baseline cost of current staff must be manually entered. Adding a connection to the museum's human resources system allows the museum to populate current pay data without manual entry. Not only does this save time, but it avoids mistakes. The payroll projection will also be more accurate because the connectivity ensures the latest information is in the tool whenever employees receive pay raises.

Some tools may benefit from integration with multiple systems. Consider a budgeting tool in which budget owners populate their budget templates for the upcoming year. Similar to the payroll tool, the budgeting tool can be integrated with the human resources system to populate current pay data, so a budget owner does not have to enter this information for every current employee. Logic can apply budget formulation guidance levels for salary and benefits inflation. With these connections, the personnel part of their spending plan has mostly been done for them. The budget owner can just focus on adjustments from the status quo, like requests for new positions or promotions.

In addition to planning expenses, budget formulation requires knowing the funding available to match uses with sources. The budgeting tool can connect to the museum's financial system to pull in data on all available funding sources and pledges expected to be received. The budgeting tool can use this data to calculate projected available fund balances for the upcoming budget year. Budget owners can see how their planned expenses consume projected available resources as they enter them.

Table 8.1 Access to Historical Data Aids Budget Owners in Creating a Realistic Spending Plan for the Upcoming Year

Line item	*Prior year budget*	*Prior year actual*	*Planned expense*
Archivist contract	$200,000	$125,000	$150,000

Source: Ashley Amos.

This connection to the financial system can also provide prior year actual expenses. The tool can populate a side-by-side view of last year's budgeted expenses, last year's actual expenses, and the upcoming year's planned expenses. This comparison is a valuable reference point as the budget owner makes decisions about how much to budget for the upcoming year.

Perhaps the budget owners see that a planned expense was budgeted at $200,000 but executed only $125,000. The budget owner can pair this information with what they know about the future of this expense (is this work expected to ramp up, wind down, or stay the same?). Rather than simply repeating the $200,000 amount that was in last year's budget, the budget owner may choose to plan for a more conservative $150,000 and use the savings to support another planned expense. Having all this data in a consolidated view—rather than having to hunt through different systems—sets this museum on a path to more realistic budgeting.

Establishing a connection between a tool and other systems that works in both directions can further integrate data sets. Keeping with our example of the budgeting tool, the museum can also leverage the interface with the financial system to share budget data with the system that houses spending data. The finance office can build logic in the financial system that alerts when an unauthorized transaction exceeds the budgeted amount for a particular funding source or office. For example, if our budget owner had budgeted the $150,000 item as their only planned expense using Fund A, the system would flag when the budget owner makes an obligation for $200,000, exceeding their authorized budget for this funding source. The connection between the two data sources enables prompt action and minimizes financial irregularities that require extra work to correct after the fact.

Reporting

When a tool makes data accessible, calculates new data using logic, and brings in additional data by interfacing with multiple systems, it is safe to say it is now a sizable data set. Sorting through this newly created mountain of data would be tedious without reporting capabilities.

Financial systems enable museums to create various types of codes to categorize transactions. These strings of numbers represent information such as the fund being used, the responsible office, and the type of purchase. Other information like project names or related strategic plan goals and objectives may also be tagged to a transaction. All of these codes lend greater context to the transaction that can later be used to support the sorting and filtering of data for reporting.

Donor reporting creates frequent needs to report financial data in different ways. Whether through established reporting schedules or because the donor reaches out with an inquiry, a museum must be prepared to quickly respond with how much of the donor's gift is still available and the areas of work the gift supported.

A user can filter and sort using the financial codes to narrow the data set to the specific fund the donor is asking about. The results may be dozens or hundreds of transactions that need to be grouped and summarized into a format suitable for sharing with the donor. Instead, if this system has a built-in reporting capability, the museum can design standard report templates that create a summary data table. All the user has to do is select the fund. When responsiveness is critical to donor stewardship, this time savings is invaluable. Further, the museum can feel confident in the accuracy of the reporting because manual filtering and summarizing did not leave room for user error.

A museum can use this same approach if reporting on a project rather than a funding source. Suppose a new exhibit is being planned that is using funds from multiple sources: the government, an individual private donor, and a corporate foundation. A financial code can be created that tags all transactions associated with this project regardless of the funding source being applied. The museum can use the financial system's reporting capability to build a project-specific report that shows how all funding sources are contributing to the overall initiative.

Donor relationships are not the only time-sensitive need for financial reporting. Returning to our budgeting tool example, this museum uses its budgeting tool not just for formulation, but also to monitor budget execution throughout the year. We discussed in the budgeting chapter the importance of subtracting commitments, obligations, and expenses from the total budget to understand how much of the budget remains available to spend throughout the year. The tool is already connected to the financial system to bring in prior year expenses, so it can also be programmed to share current year spending. Without this connection, employees would need to export their budget from the budgeting tool and their spending from the financial system to manually compare the data sets in a spreadsheet.

The budgeting tool can be used to build a report that connects these data sets and summarizes them to the level needed by users. This reporting provides a consolidated view of how the museum is executing against its budget. A real-time interface means that every time a bill is paid, the report will instantly update to show a decrease in the remaining budget. Multiple versions of budget execution reporting can be built to meet different needs or provide more or less detail based on the role of the user. For example, an office head may need a very high-level summary while their office administrator needs to monitor budget execution more closely.

Visualization

For those who respond better to visualizations than tables, dashboards can also be created to report on summary data using charts. In our risk management example, this tool has the capability to chart key performance indicator data, rather than the risk owner needing to create these in a separate application. Looking beyond the individual risk level, the tool can also plot all museum risks on a quad chart based on their assigned likelihood and impact. The CRO need not worry about exporting data from the tool to produce the quad chart before each governance meeting.

Returning to our budgeting tool example, recall that this museum wants to track budget execution in the tool. The tool's visualization capability includes a gauge that compares the time remaining in the budget year with the amount of budget that remains unspent. This can be a quick indicator of whether spending is going too fast—risking that funds will be depleted before end of year—or too slow—risking that expiring funds will be unutilized. When the museum begins to see a major deviation between the gauge needles, it can dig into more detailed reports or transaction-level data to identify the cause.

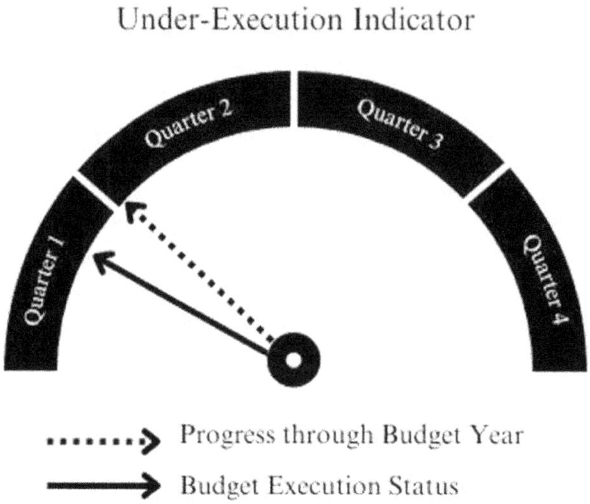

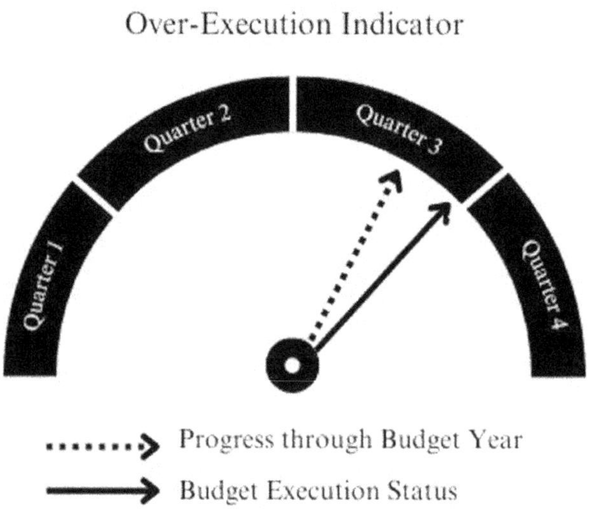

Figure 8.2 Gauges Measure Budget Execution Progress throughout the Year. *Source*: Ashley Amos.

Visualizations can be useful to see trends in complex data sets over time. A cash forecasting tool is designed to help a museum manage and optimize its cash flow. This means tracking and forecasting cash inflows and outflows. Cash management ensures there is enough cash in the bank to pay for the museum's day-to-day operational costs. Effective cash management will also enable a museum to invest any surplus cash that exceeds operating needs to maximize its financial position.

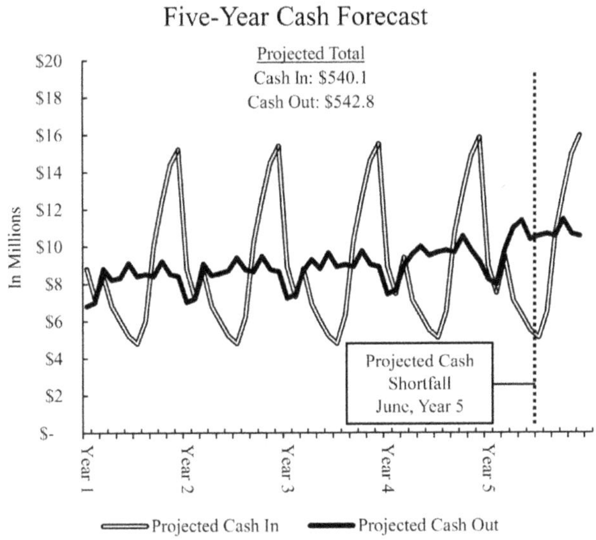

Figure 8.3 Chart Forecasting Cash Availability over Five Years. *Source*: Ashley Amos.

Let's say a museum wants to build a cash forecasting tool with a five-year outlook. Projecting available cash over this long period requires the analysis of numerous inputs. Historical monthly cash inflows and outflows provide a baseline for how much cash the museum has available each month. Assumptions can be applied to projected cash outflows, with cost inflation applied to the cost of personnel, goods, and services. Future fundraising and new spending above historical levels can be layered into the calculation. A museum that engages in multi-year budgeting will already have much of this information for future years.

Revenue collection and the payment of expenses at any museum will vary month to month, but review of historical trends can identify seasonal patterns that repeat each year. Perhaps donations peak near the end of the tax year or several large annual contracts are paid at the start of the budget year. Logic can be programmed into the cash forecasting tool to account for these recurring ebbs and flows.

This many variables make for a complex spreadsheet, but this information can all be captured in the back end of the would tool and represented to users through a summary visualization. Displaying the data of a five-year period in a chart format will more easily alert users to patterns and trends than a large table. Let's say the finance office has populated the tool and observes that both revenue and spending have followed predictable cycles in recent years, with certain months representing high and low seasons. They can use this chart to quickly pinpoint when those fluctuations are expected to result in a cash deficit because more cash has gone out the door than come in.

While the chart shows that cash outflows are expected to exceed cash inflows during certain times of year, the museum is able to maintain a positive cash position because of accumulated cash reserves. However, the museum is projected to end the five-year forecast in a negative cash position. By June of that year, the museum will not have enough cash in the bank to pay its bills. Early detection enables the museum to take action far in advance of this projected cash shortfall. The summary visualization and its underlying assumptions can be shared with museum leaders to prompt discussion of a new fundraising campaign, changes to planned spending, or outside financing options.

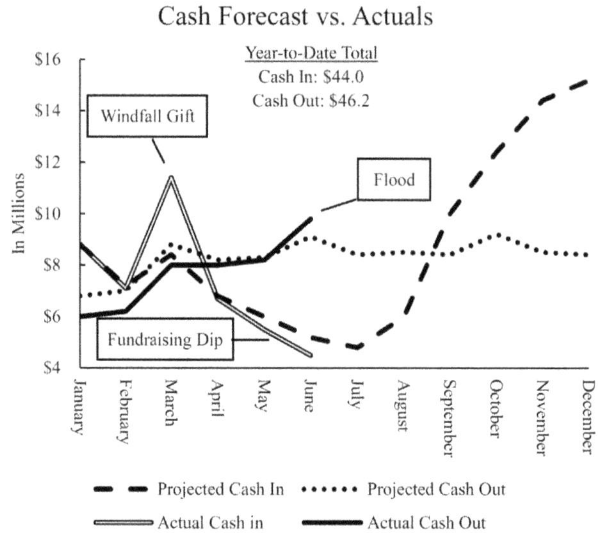

Figure 8.4 Chart Comparing Forecasted Cash to Actual Cash during Budget Year. *Source*: Ashley Amos.

This museum's cash forecast can also provide input for scenario planning. If next year's cash position looks strong, that may inform a budget increase scenario. Low cash may prompt a budget decrease scenario. The museum can make resource allocation decisions now that can be acted upon if the forecast comes to fruition.

The museum can also review the cash forecast against actual performance. The forecast projects cash inflows and outflows for the twelve months of the budget year, and each month new data of actual cash inflows and outflows will become available. The museum can chart how its actual performance compares to its forecast to monitor whether its cash position is playing out as expected.

Imagine this museum had a stronger than expected first quarter for fundraising, in particular due to an unexpected $3 million gift received in March. Spending in this first quarter is tracking lower than expected, further enhancing the museum's positive cash position. By spring, the museum is beginning to fall short of projected fundraising, and a flood in the archives prompted remediation and repair bills that exceeded planned spending in June. The combined effect of these deviations from the projection puts the museum in a negative cash position, requiring it to draw on its cash reserves or sell investments to free up more cash. If the museum hits its cash goals for the fundraising high season in the last quarter, it should still end the year in a positive cash position. The remainder of the budget year will need to be closely monitored to prevent this short-term cash flow problem from getting more than just the museum's archives under water.

Choosing the Right Financial Tools

Selecting a financial tool is about more than the capabilities the tool comes equipped with, but also the capacity of the museum to incorporate the tool into its working environment. There is no one-size-fits-all financial tool for any museum. Museums will have different goals they

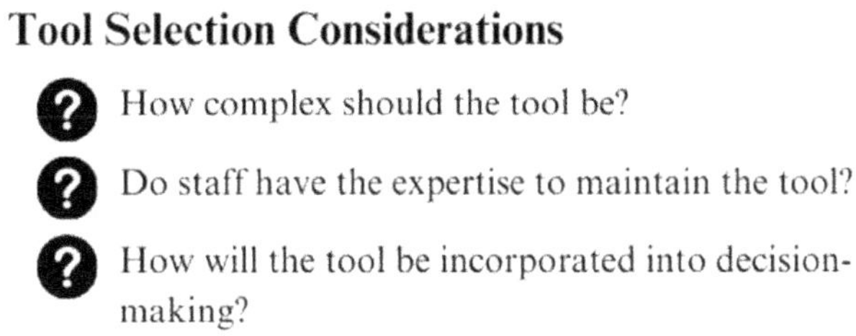

Figure 8.5 Considerations for Selecting Financial Tools. *Source*: Ashley Amos.

are trying to achieve with financial tools, requiring different capabilities. Each museum will also have financial limitations regarding the cost to purchase and maintain a financial tool.

Which financial tools are adopted will also depend on the museum's progress in other building blocks of FIRM. A museum embarking on risk management may want to incorporate a tool in that process from the start, rather than beginning the process in disparate spreadsheet templates and moving to a software solution later. A museum steadily advancing current budgeting processes will evaluate the right timing to add a budgeting tool or replace an outdated one. A museum can select the right tool for its needs by considering three key factors: complexity, staff expertise, and decision-making.

Complexity

Complexity considers how the selected tool will operate to carry out the museum's goal. A tool is only as good as the data within the system. If the tool requires data inputs that are not readily available or exceed current capabilities, the museum may be signing itself up for labor-intensive efforts to generate new data to populate the tool. Significant manual effort to input and upkeep data undercuts the value of tools derived from programming logic and connectivity.

Even when the needed data is available in another system, a lack of connectivity can complicate the smooth functioning of the tool. A museum considering a tool will want to identify the data sources early so it selects the option that interfaces best with existing systems. Perhaps a museum can purchase an add-on from the provider of its financial system that enables direct, real-time integration. Another tool on the market may have more desirable features, but will require more manual uploads of data. The museum may regret the lack of data connection down the road when day-to-day operation of the tool becomes burdensome.

Just because a financial tool has the functionality to be complex, it doesn't mean all that functionality is needed by a particular museum. A tool may have a wide array of customization options that can be programmed to a museum's specifications. A museum that is not very clear on the functionality it is trying to achieve may unintentionally over-build the tool. It may have purchased the tool with the intent of solving one problem, but in its excitement it begins to layer in more and more related problems the tool could help with. The customized tool may become too unwieldy to program, too bogged down with data to run smoothly, and too large for users to confidently navigate. It is important to maintain focus on what the museum is trying to achieve, rather than adding unnecessary bells and whistles that may make the tool more cumbersome and less useful in the end.

Staff Expertise

Scaling complexity goes hand-in-hand with the capabilities of museum staff—both those responsible for programming and operating the tool and the wider group who will be users of the tool. Implementation of financial tools relies heavily on change management and financial literacy.

Adopting new financial tools may sound daunting or intimidating to those who are used to current ways of doing business. Employees with experience using financial tools may have flashbacks to botched system implementations. These future users need to be engaged early and often during the selection and development of the tool. When it is time to roll out the tool to users, the appropriate level of training and documentation must be in place for various user communities. Users may need ongoing training and support as they learn how to incorporate the tool into their daily work.

A budgeting tool that requires wide adoption across the museum will require a much more significant change management process compared to a payroll projection tool that is used only by the finance office. The rollout of the payroll tool can be more narrowly focused to the individual financial literacy of the small number of staff who will use it to carry out their work.

Tools may have varying capabilities that don't need to be deployed all at once. Perhaps a museum's change management strategy begins with the simplest aspects of the tool. The museum focuses first on familiarizing users with the tool through data entry practices and ensuring users understand how to interpret any data pulled in from other systems. Then the museum adds layers of logic, reporting, and visualization to demonstrate to users how the tool can make calculations easier and provide useful views of their data. Examples like payroll projection and cash management tools can be deployed on an annual or multi-year scale based on how advanced a museum has become in multi-year planning.

Last, but not least, tools need to be maintained by museum staff. Glitches or bugs in the software can lead to incorrect calculations or loss of data. A change management process and data log needs to be included in the tool that ensures system changes are appropriately approved and documented. The IT software landscape changes rapidly, impacting not just functionality but the museum's IT security posture. Software updates to the tool or related systems might lead to future integration problems. Data stored in the system and connection points to other systems must be protected consistent with the museum's privacy policies, especially relating to sensitive data like employee salaries.

It is essential to ensure a clear division of responsibility between the IT office and the tool owner about various aspects of system maintenance. Employees will come and go, but the financial tool will remain. Staff turnover should not make a tool obsolete. Perhaps a museum relies on a single employee in the finance office who has become the expert on the financial tool. Other employees defer to them because they have led the programming from the beginning. It is imperative that this employee document the actions they undertake for system upkeep and train other employees so institutional knowledge is not lost.

Perhaps a museum lacks the staff expertise to implement a new financial tool. The museum should determine at the time of purchase whether the software vendor can provide support personnel to help build the system to the museum's needs. These functions can be transitioned to museum staff once the tool is operational, or continued as an ongoing cost of maintaining the tool. When support services are not offered as part of the software purchase, the museum may be able to separately contract with a vendor who has expertise in the platform.

Decision-Making

Financial tools help museum leaders make faster decisions in a changing environment. The ability to plan, prepare, and make timely decisions leads to a more resilient museum. However, tools cannot solve financial problems by themselves. If a museum relies too heavily on its tools, this can lead to a lack of personal engagement with financial decisions.

Tools must support rather than supplant decision-making. Museum leaders should not blindly heed a tool's insights by effectively delegating decision-making to the tool. It is very easy to fall into the trap that a tool will always have the right answer. This complacency can lead to poor financial decisions or lack of oversight. A false sense of security may impair critical thinking. Financial tools are just one input that can support museum leaders. Strategic decisions need to be made with both programmatic and financial information.

At the other extreme is the risk that museum leaders distrust a tool because its logic is not well documented or its forecasts don't align with their own personal predictions. An aspect of change management must focus on museum leaders and governance members who may not be direct users of the tool but will be recipients of its analysis, reports, or visualizations. Leaders need to have sufficient understanding of a tool to not question its accuracy or validity when presented with its outputs.

If a museum can strike the right balance between overreliance and skepticism, financial tools can be of great value when combined with other quantitative and qualitative sources to support decision-making.

INCORPORATING ARTIFICIAL INTELLIGENCE

Artificial Intelligence (AI) refers to the simulation of human intelligence in machines that are designed to think, learn, and perform tasks that typically require human intelligence.[1] These tasks can include problem-solving, understanding natural language, recognizing patterns, and making decisions. AI works by aggregating massive amounts of data for the user, sometimes when being prompted to provide an answer to a simple question. Generative AI, which is a form of AI, creates new content, including text, videos, images, and audio. It is assuming the probability of the outcome that the user requests and creating a new product.

AI is already being used in many parts of our daily lives. When we use the GPS in our cars or phones, AI is making real-time decisions for our trips. Digital assistants, commonly called chatbots, are popping every time we use our computers or phones to order a product, pay a bill, or schedule a service.

AI will continue to evolve and dramatically change how we live and how museums operate. An AI project called Fragmentarium is being led by the University of Munich to piece together as many as a half a million clay tablets to complete a 3,000-year-old story.[2] Machines, not humans, are leading the way with this initiative in an attempt to complete a version of the poem, the Epic of Gilgamesh, from the Mesopotamian collections of various world museums and universities.[3] Without AI, a project of this magnitude would take several generations to complete.[4]

However, AI is fraught with risks. One concern for museums is what are termed hallucinations.[5] These are incorrect results generated by AI that be caused by bad data, insufficient training, or biases in the model.[6] A museum that uses and disseminates factually incorrect information would never be able to recover its reputation to the public and its stakeholders. Other risks include the perception that employees may be replaced by machines and the lack of human engagement may lead to a loss in internal and external communication channels.

If a museum chooses to use some form of AI, they must also consider how to integrate AI into their institution in an organized manner. This starts with governance, which establishes a museum-wide policy and standard operating procedures for the use of AI. Museum leadership needs to be very specific with which versions of AI are acceptable for internal use.

This effort can be very time-consuming because an AI tool that may work for the finance team may not serve the education or collections teams. The creation and delivery of content from a machine is a very different application than the use of AI for patching computers or providing accounting support. Finding the right equilibrium is made more difficult by the speed at which the technology is evolving.

At a museum, AI may be used to aggregate large amounts of data to write curriculum. It can be used to match photos in the collection and even mine the collection for a particular word or phrase. All of these manual tasks that were formerly performed by staff can now be done by machines.

Museums may already be applying AI to help secure its digital collections. For example, museums have thousands of active informational technology access points and digital assets. Each of these points needs to be regularly maintained for access, compliance, and security. A logic can be written which can gather this data and identify the network points that are most vulnerable for a cyber intrusion. This information could then be used to create a strategy to close these vulnerabilities from the most to least risky access points. This strategy would then be augmented by an automated tool which would be responsible for the patch management of these access points.

AI will present many opportunities to advance financial management at a museum. This can mean creating a strategy for how staff perform financial work and how they interact with internal and external stakeholders. One approach could be focusing only on back office operations. AI as a financial tool will allow a museum to automate repetitive tasks. Transaction tracking, bill payments, and investment monitoring are all tasks that can be transitioned from employees to automated tools. This can save time and resources and eliminate human errors. However, the decision to use AI should not be made solely for financial efficiency. Stakeholder expectations need to be considered.

Using chatbots to reduce the interaction between the finance team and its internal customers would change how the museum communicates within its walls. For example, museum staff working on financial reports or looking for a particular piece of data may no longer need to make a call or send an email for information. All of this interaction can happen in a matter of seconds with a chatbot. But does the museum want to create distance between its internal customers and the finance office? Will important nuances be lost and relationships that depend on constant communication suffer?

Personal financial relationships extend outside the museum. Would the museum want to reduce its in-person relationships with its vendors and donors? This must also be considered when implementing a chatbot for external communication. Vendors inquiring about a payment would no longer make numerous calls to find the status of their invoice. However, a vendor may need an immediate answer from the museum and having to navigate a chatbot may create unnecessary delays in both communication and service delivery.

Sometimes pledge payments are late or do not arrive. AI can be used to send out invoices and reminders to donors who may be behind on payments. However, a donor may become frustrated by the lack of personal contact. They may find the reminder from an automated service offensive and want to speak with a representative of the development office.

FIRM CONNECTIONS

Whether financial tools are used for short- or long-term planning and forecasting, they enable museums to more easily adopt a forward-looking posture. The other building blocks of the Resilience pillar—risk management, scenario planning, and multi-year budgeting—are all enabled by the adoption of financial tools that leverage the power of data, analysis, and user-friendly outputs. Annual budgeting and strategic planning processes also achieve greater integration from financial tools that centralize information and reduce the need for labor-intensive calculations. The increasing technical sophistication of financial tool solutions—and the advancement of financial literacy they promote—requires museums to continually assess how new capabilities can be deployed to further their pursuit of financial health and stability.

Chapter 9

Scenario Planning

RESILIENCE BUILDING BLOCK 3

Scenario planning is the third building block of the Resilience pillar. Whether envisioning the upcoming year or multiple years into the future, scenario planning challenges museum leaders to think about how they would respond when faced with a shifting environment. Information gleaned from other FIRM capabilities such as budgeting, risk management, and financial tools can facilitate the design of scenarios that leaders want to prepare for. A strong culture of governance and change management enables a museum to make holistic decisions and navigate dynamic environments without being pulled off course in its strategic endeavors. This chapter will explore how museums can design, plan for, and make decisions in advance about alternative future scenarios as an extension of the budgeting process.

Part of building resilience is being prepared for the future, as institutions increasingly need to quickly respond to changes in an uncertain and complex environment. Without a crystal ball, how can an institution prepare itself for what's coming?

Strategic planning is one way to look to the future. A strategy outlines an imagined future and leverages what an institution knows about its strengths and weaknesses and its opportunities and threats to help navigate its environment to reach the desired future state. A strategic plan keeps an institution focused in a concerted direction, but can be thrown off course by unexpected—likely external—forces that arise during its lifespan.

Risk management is another way to look to the future. By identifying risks and taking steps to manage them, an institution can smooth its future path. Risk identification is limited by the collective imagination of an institution. Only those risks that are known can be managed, and an even smaller subset of risks will have a high enough likelihood and impact to assign limited resources to manage. There may be many other potential challenges that could befall an institution that are unaddressed or unknown.

Scenario planning offers a different approach. Scenario planning asks the institution to expand its understanding by considering multiple potential futures. Defined scenarios stimulate thinking about how an institution would react if the potential future occurs. There are many types of scenarios that can be developed for different types of uncertainties: economic, political, technological, and societal, among others. Scenarios may be long or short term, general or specific, and simple or complex.

Scenario planning traces its roots back to military strategy. Herman Kahn, a RAND Corporation analyst, developed a technique for pairing imagined stories with the analytical rigor usually reserved for real-world problems.[1] During the Cold War era, Kahn applied this technique to explore potential outcomes of nuclear war.[2]

At the same time, other practitioners began applying similar techniques to the business sector. Companies started to contemplate the effects of scenarios such as natural disasters, global pandemics, and geopolitical shifts. Shell envisioned decades-long scenarios to help it navigate uncertainties in the global energy market.[3] These scenario planning efforts have been credited with positioning Shell to be the most prepared in its industry for the multiple oil crises that ensued during the 1970s and 1980s.[4] Museums that are increasing their institutional financial literacy can use planning exercises to have responses ready for both short-term (annual) and significant (multi-year) changes to their financial landscape. Valuable time and resources will not be lost trying to gauge the impact of sudden changes, many will have been already effectively documented.

Long-term and elaborate scenario planning can be very resource intensive. It is reasonable to assume that few outside of the Fortune 500 or government research institutions would have the ability to rigorously pursue such an endeavor. In the context of FIRM, the use of scenario planning is scaled down to be supportable in a nonprofit environment and narrowed to focus on financial stability. Short- to mid-term financial scenarios require a less intensive planning process while still providing instructive insights about the future.

Unanticipated financial circumstances for museums take many forms. In 2024, the University of New Hampshire faced a campus-wide budget deficit of $14 million.[5] The university made the decision to close its Museum of Art as part of necessary budget cuts, noting that the museum could only be sustained if it were supported by donors rather than university funding.[6]

In 2021, Amazon founder Jeff Bezos donated $200 million to the Smithsonian Institute—the largest gift since its founding.[7] The donation allowed the Smithsonian to renovate the National Air and Space Museum and construct a new education center.[8] Such a large gift was certainly not anticipated in the institution's budget, but it had to be prepared to carry out the massive projects once the gift was received.[9]

BENEFITS OF SCENARIO PLANNING

Scenario planning helps a museum prepare for the ups and downs that may be in its financial future before they come to be. The goal is not to accurately predict the future but to enhance the museum's ability to make decisions in a changing world. For institutions with well-established goals, scenario planning can be a way to anticipate the future, to gain a sense of control, or to make incremental improvements over time. For institutions with less defined goals, scenario planning functions as a learning tool and can help clarify what their goals are.

Scenario planning helps an institution improve its decision-making. The planning process creates a structured venue for decision-makers to evaluate problems and select their preferred response in advance. Decision-makers have the time and space to consider how different responses to a scenario may impact the institution and its future.

Scenario planning makes an institution more adaptable to future changes. Once a decision has been made about how the institution will respond to a given scenario, the solution is sitting on a shelf ready to be dusted off if a real challenge arises. The institution is able to pivot more quickly than if it had to create a solution out of thin air.

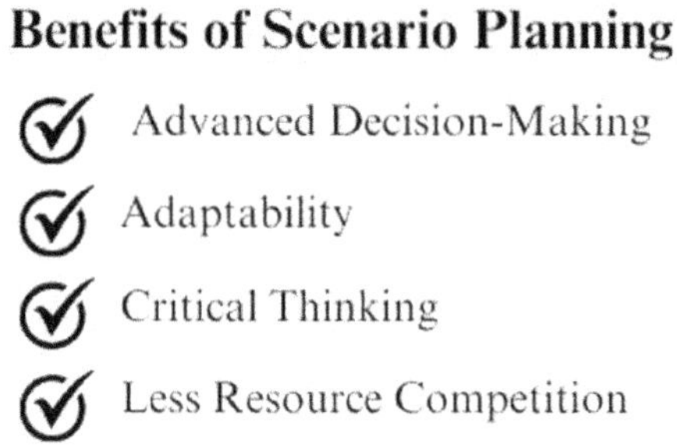

Figure 9.1 Benefits of Scenario Planning. *Source*: Ashley Amos.

Scenario planning stimulates critical thinking by contributing to a culture that values advanced planning and prioritization. The reality is that no institution can control its future or do everything it plans to do. A culture built on regularly exercising scenarios will be better prepared when—not if—things don't go their way and is more confident in having thoroughly considered its approach in advance.

Finally, scenario planning encourages an institution-wide mindset. Rather than offices being protective or territorial about their own resources, the structured process gives everyone an opportunity to make their case to leadership before a decision is made about the best path forward for the entire museum. The impulse to compete is lessened by the hypothetical nature of the exercise.

FIRM CONNECTIONS: BUDGETING AND GOVERNANCE

The budgeting chapter emphasized that a budget is just a plan. The plan is made months ahead of the budget year, which plays out over another twelve months. Accurately predicting both the funding sources and expenses that will exist at the end of the budget year is nearly impossible. Building a revision schedule into the budget cycle helps ensure that the plan does not get out of step with reality.

Even with the ability to revise the budget, budget execution expects the institution to adapt to changing circumstances as they take shape. Perhaps a source of funding is no longer expected to reach the level anticipated in the budget. Offices that rely on this source begin to worry about how the shortage will impact them. Leaders compete to protect their interests in the limited funds that are available. Employees feel uncertainty about how the new funding reality will impact them.

Strong governance over the budget process can mitigate some of the chaos and uneasiness of budget execution. Governance provides a venue for all the options to be presented and considered through defined decision processes. But the museum still needs to make immediate decisions about what to cut from the budget to address its funding shortage. Offices scramble to put together their proposals and make their case to governance. Until the decision process plays out, time ticks by and the museum has not yet altered its course.

The museum can mitigate the immediacy of these budget execution decisions by planning for them. No one can anticipate every potential eventuality, but likely scenarios can be considered in advance. Scenario planning seeks to get ahead of these budget execution

Figure 9.2 Scenario Planning Steps. *Source*: Ashley Amos.

challenges by asking governance to consider them before they occur. If a budget is a plan, then the scenarios examine what the museum would do if the year doesn't go according to plan.

The work of scenario planning occurs during budget formulation. As part of formulation, the finance office prepares budget guidance that includes information on how much funding is expected to be available. Offices are then tasked with populating a budget template by identifying and prioritizing their planned expenses to fit within the projected funding level. Scenario planning expands budget formulation guidance by asking offices to brainstorm how they would adjust their budget request if the projected funding level changed. In addition to completing the budget template, offices are asked to make a resource allocation plan in response to each scenario.

SCENARIO CONSTRUCTION

Now that we have fixed scenario planning's position within the budget process, we can explore how these scenarios are developed. There are a few considerations for a museum embarking on a scenario planning effort, beginning with determining the key issues the museum wants to test. Ideal scenarios encourage inquiry, challenge assumptions, and ensure the status quo is not taken for granted.

It is important to limit the number of scenarios that will be included in budget formulation guidance. Choose only a few—asking each office to plan for ten scenarios at once would be overwhelming. Scenarios should not be too complicated or require multiple interdependent assumptions. Such imagined futures can start to sound farfetched and become very time-consuming to design and plan for.

Scenario building generally involves three steps: identifying information as inputs, processing that information through analysis or modeling, and using the output to construct a specific scenario. How rigorous an institution may be in applying these three steps depends on its level of financial literacy. Progress in the other FIRM areas of budgeting, strategic planning, risk management, financial tools, and multi-year budgeting will also impact how much information and analytical capability a museum can apply to scenario construction.

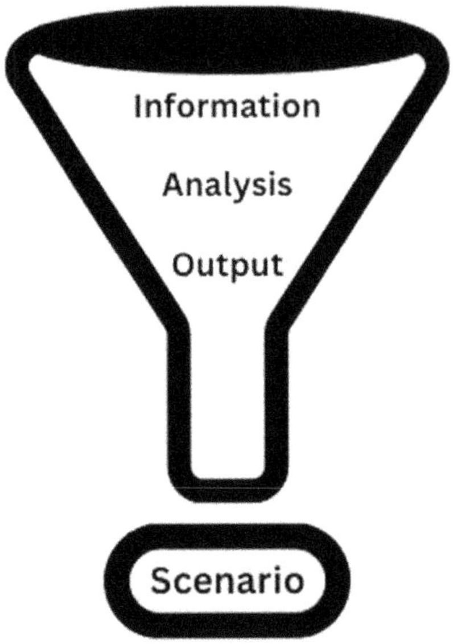

Figure 9.3 How to Build a Scenario. *Source*: Ashley Amos.

Simple scenario planning involves applying percentage increases and decreases to the current budget level. The finance office can create these scenarios based on available financial data. Historical revenue can be analyzed to understand trends or input into financial models to forecast future revenue. Finance may also consult with the fundraising office to understand if certain revenue goals are becoming harder to meet or if they are seeing a shift in the donor pool.

Finance can use the outputs of its analysis to establish a range of potential budget changes. Perhaps they choose 5 and 10 percent as their scenarios for budget increases and decreases. Another museum experiencing greater financial volatility may choose a broader range, perhaps 8 and 15 percent. A museum with a relatively steady environment may elect for narrower scenarios of 2 and 5 percent. The guidance for each percentage scenario tasks offices to identify the items they would add to or subtract from their budget request in response to the percentage change in projected funding level.

Alternatively, a museum may have more sophisticated information and analysis available to support more specific scenarios. Imagine in this example that the finance office assembles representatives from across the museum to design scenarios. Collaboration with the owners of other data sets expands the amount of information from which to develop scenarios and contributes additional analytic capability.

Perhaps the development office is worried about a specific type of funding: a multi-year grant that may not be renewed. At the same time, the government relations team is monitoring potential legislative action that would decrease the museum's public funding sources.

Internal factors should not be ignored in the exploration of information. The human resources office shares staffing information that indicates a wave of retirements may be coming, providing significant payroll savings if eligible employees depart. Perhaps the strategic planning lead identifies a major project that is on the verge of project overruns. The additional funds may need to be shifted to the project since it supports a top strategic priority.

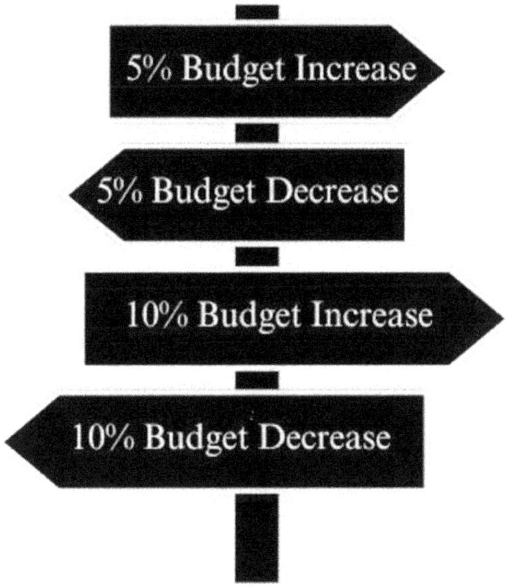

Figure 9.4 Simple Scenario Examples. *Source*: Ashley Amos.

Specific scenarios provide a greater practical benefit because they spark more insights for decision-makers. For example, in the scenario of a $5-million grant not being renewed, the simple solution—and the one most likely to occur if the grant suddenly disappears during budget execution—is that the project supported by the grant stops work. However, by tasking offices across the institution with this scenario in advance, budget governance could consider multiple options. If they want to ensure the project continues despite the uncertainty of the grant, they can decide to divert resources from other work to fill this $5 million void.

The same budget execution challenges hold true when the unexpected budget change is seemingly positive. Perhaps a windfall gift could provide unanticipated opportunities for new, expanded, or expedited work. A museum can waste valuable time identifying and initiating new work after a gift is received. The donor wants to be able to see progress and impact within the first year.

Advanced consideration of the windfall scenario enables budget governance to know what investments would be next in line for funding. Connections between budget governance and strategic planning governance will also ensure the investment decision aligns with top strategic priorities.

The most advanced approach to scenario construction can occur in institutions with multi-year budget processes. Annual budgeting may feel like a heavy lift due to its level of detail, but it is still very short-term planning. A scenario may assume revenue drops in the upcoming budget year but doesn't consider what happens if the change persists or worsens in the years that follow. A museum with an established capacity for multi-year thinking may incorporate scenario planning that envisions larger-scale scenarios that unfold over multiple budget years. Offices are asked to use projections and modeling to consider the multi-year impact of their proposed efficiencies, cuts, or investments.

A multi-year approach is especially valuable when considering the impact of scenarios on staffing. In a budget decrease scenario, offices may only be able to achieve the needed savings by terminating staff whose projects will be stopped. However, the scenario does not consider

Figure 9.5 Specific Scenario Examples. *Source*: Ashley Amos.

whether the need for savings is short-lived. Those staff may be needed for the next year's budget priorities and cannot easily be rehired or replaced if the museum's financial outlook changes. A museum that considers the impact of scenarios alongside existing multi-year budgeting and strategic planning activities will have a better understanding of the long-term impacts of short-term solutions.

The same logic holds true for budget increase scenarios. Multi-year scenario planning helps articulate the spending tail of an investment made in the first year. Consider an office that proposes additional funding be used to start a new project, including hiring new personnel to carry it out. Unless these employees are hired for a specified term, they may continue being museum employees once the project is complete. This response to a short-term funding increase will balloon payroll costs long after a one-year budget scenario has ended.

RESOURCE ALLOCATION PLANS

Once scenarios are designed, the finance office distributes them as part of budget formulation guidance. Offices are provided templates they will use to outline their resource allocation plan in response to each scenario.

The template for resource allocation plans should include opportunities to share both quantitative and qualitative information about the plan's impact. For example, a proposal to cut or expand a project will include details about the change in project scope and updated project milestones. The plan can also highlight interdependencies with other projects to fully represent the effects. Most importantly, the plan should articulate how the proposed change impacts the institution's strategic plan.

Quantitative data should include not just the change in financial resources, but also personnel and time. Expansion of a project may require additional staff and associated hiring support from the human resources office. Descoping a project may give back the time of current employees. This time savings may not reduce payroll costs, but would allow the museum to transfer the excess employee time to other work areas. In the event of more extreme cuts, the plan can identify positions to be eliminated. Any change in personnel can also share a qualitative assessment such as lost skill sets or morale impact.

The template is only a valuable means of information collection to the extent offices take the exercise seriously. Budget governance has an important role to play in setting the tone for the effort. Each office should be expected to provide a comprehensive set of resource allocation plans in response to the scenarios. None should be exempted from responding or allowed to provide perfunctory responses.

If one office takes a hard look at painful cuts, another cannot be allowed to shrug off the scenario. The uncooperative office may respond that they could not find much, if anything at all, to cut. Or they may employ the so-called Washington Monument strategy.[10] Named for the phenomenon in which government agencies like the National Park Service volunteer to eliminate their highest visibility service, budget owners propose a cut knowing full well that the plan would never be approved.[11] Governance must emphasize a mindset of anticipating solutions rather than justifying the status quo.

A small office may be asked to respond to a 5 percent budget reduction scenario that amounts to a $2 million cut to the museum's budget. However, this small office's entire budget is only $1.5 million. The office would certainly not be expected to propose its own dismantling in its resource allocation plan. However, governance should make clear that they expect a good faith effort to identify any internal changes that can contribute to the museum-wide scenario.

Perhaps this office derives cost savings through a proposed efficiency or elimination of a contract that amounts to $200,000. Or the office may propose austerity measures that cut its $1.5 million budget by 5 percent across the board. The amount will fall short of the total reduction needed museum-wide but can be combined with other offices' plans to fully address the $2 million scenario.

Similarly, this small office may be asked to respond to a scenario that assumes museum funding increases by $2 million. It is unlikely that the office has a realistic proposal for more than doubling its current $1.5 million budget. Instead, a good faith effort may propose a $250,000 increase that would double the resources for an ongoing project. The office can make the case that speeding up the project's deliverable will allow the museum to engage in ongoing public discourse about an issue. The opportunity may have passed by the project's current completion timeline and would not be possible without the additional resources.

By ensuring the office's response stays grounded in its current workload and capabilities, it may receive a more favorable response from budget governance. The modest amount of the plan also increases the likelihood of success, as it can easily be combined with the plans of other offices to total the $2 million increase.

RESOURCE ALLOCATION DECISIONS

Budget governance is responsible for approving spending plans submitted by offices at the budget formulation deadline. Governance members are expected to take an institutional perspective rather than just representing their role. This can be a challenging vantage point to maintain when reviewing the funding request for an office they oversee.

Adding scenario planning to budget formulation makes the task of budget governance even more thorny. Governance must now also evaluate the offices and projects they are close to for cuts that can feel drastic. They must be able to put their individual connections aside to collectively determine which resource allocation plan (or combination of plans) will be adopted as the institution's decision for each scenario.

Resource allocation plans may take different paths depending on the budget formulation process at an institution. The first option is to send all offices' plans to budget governance for consideration. This option is better for smaller museums without a large number of offices. The prospect of reviewing dozens of proposals for the same scenario may be overwhelming. However, this approach maximizes the opportunity for governance to consider all available options.

Alternatively, offices can submit their resource allocation plans to their executive leader, who then selects their preferred resource allocation plan to represent their segment of the institution. This approach may mirror existing spending plan approval procedures, in which offices coordinate their submissions through their leadership during budget formulation. The review process should help the most realistic and strategic proposals rise to the top. This option has the benefit of allowing executives who are governance members to first wear their own hat in making decisions about their offices and then transition to considering the overall best option for the institution.

In either of these paths, the finance office reviews the resource allocation plans before they are presented to budget governance. This is an opportunity to validate the financial assumptions used to prepare the plans and provide the finance office's perspective on their effectiveness. Finance may also coordinate with the lead for strategic planning to weigh in on resource allocation plans. Decisions to increase funding should reinforce top strategic planning priorities, whereas the impact of funding decrease scenarios should be limited to lower-priority work. Understanding the linkage to strategic planning can help ensure the museum is sending clear and consistent messages to staff across strategic planning, budgeting,

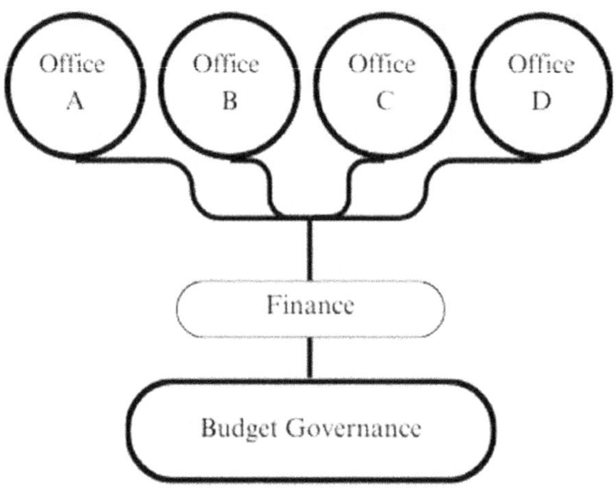

Figure 9.6 All Resource Allocation Plans Are Sent Directly to the Finance Office for Consideration by Governance. *Source*: Ashley Amos.

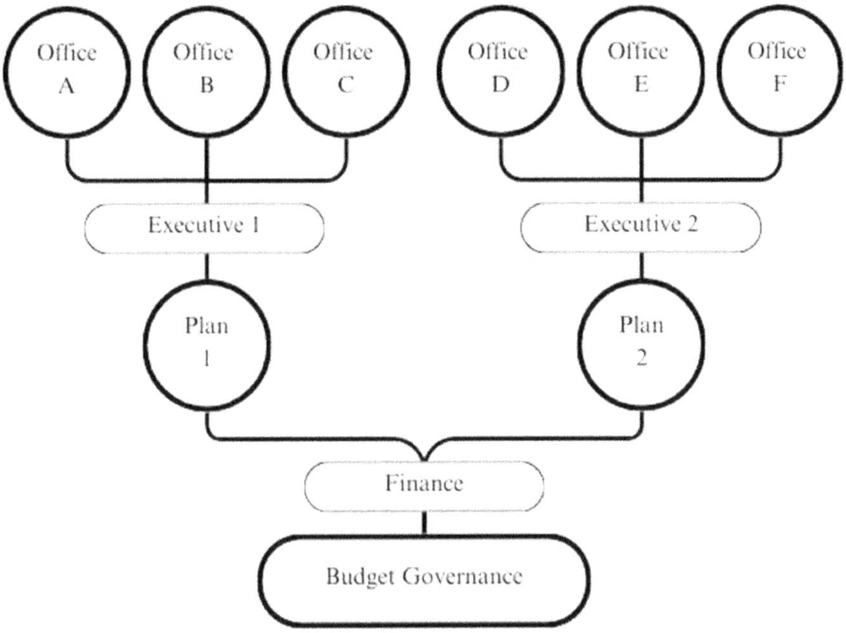

Figure 9.7 Resource Allocation Plans Are Reviewed by Executives to Determine What Moves Forward to the Finance Office and Governance. *Source*: Ashley Amos.

and scenario planning activities. These strategic planning assessments can be provided to budget governance to help guide their considerations of the resource allocation plans.

Once these perspectives have been assembled and both the draft budget and the resource allocation plans have been delivered, budget governance reviews the myriad financial decisions before them. There are three general approaches that an institution can apply to incorporate scenario planning into budgeting: focusing on the budget first, using the scenarios to make adjustments to the budget, and setting aside a portion of the budget for scenarios.

Budget First

The first and simplest approach is for budget governance to run the budget approval process as they would have before they added scenario planning. Governance evaluates and approves the budget for the upcoming year on its own and then sets it aside. Then they evaluate each scenario. With the budget having already been established as the approved plan, governance will have a better understanding of the budget impacts of each scenario. The resource allocation decision becomes about what would be done if the plan has to change.

Budget Adjustment

Another approach is to consider the draft budget and the resource allocation plans together. Recall the example of a museum that selects increase and decrease scenarios of 5 and 10 percent. Each office has been asked to respond to these prompts. As budget governance

Table 9.1 Scenario Decision Approaches.

Budget first	Approve budget, then consider scenarios as future budget changes
Budget adjustment	Use scenarios to add or subtract investments in draft budget
Budget set aside	Plan against a reduced budget, invest in scenarios within remaining funding pool

Source: Ashley Amos.

considers the draft budget the finance office has laid before them, they may want to consider changing the distribution of funds across various offices.

Governance has the tools at their disposal to envision what would happen if Office A was given a 5 percent budget increase to support a new project while Offices B and C were cut to make up the difference. All three offices have already provided governance with the information they need to make this decision. Resource allocation plans provide a suite of options that can be mixed and matched to rebalance the budget to align with institutional strategic priorities. This approach hones in on what is truly a priority while controlling the overall budget to remain within projected funding levels.

Budget Set Aside

As a hybrid of the two approaches, a museum may set aside a portion of its projected funding to consider against its budget increase scenarios. Imagine a museum with projected funding availability of $150 million. This museum's budget formulation guidance assigns a budget cap to each office totaling up to $145 million. Finance has intentionally left a $5 million gap that can be allocated by budget governance at the end of formulation.

This approach focuses primarily on budget increase scenarios. Offices have already built the necessary decreases into the draft budget by being required to fit their planned expenses within a lower budget cap. Armed with a stack of resource allocation plans, budget governance can distribute the $5 million to proposed investments without needing to offset them with decreases in other areas. The remaining resource allocation plans that are not selected for investment may still be considered for scenarios that exceed the budget, as they would in the budget first approach.

WHEN SCENARIOS MEET REALITY

Strong support of museum executives is essential not just in the scenario planning process, but to ensure the decisions made actually drive future action. Imagine a museum that planned for a scenario in which a particular grant is not received the next budget year. Offices across the museum worked in good faith to deliver resource allocation plans and budget governance carefully reached a decision about how the museum would respond. The decision was that three other projects would be partially cut to enable the grant-supported project to be completed despite the loss of the grant.

Nine months later, this scenario has become reality. The museum has been notified by the grant maker that it will not receive the funds it relied on in the budget. The leader of one of the projects slated to be cut makes a plea to be spared because the project has a lot of momentum that will be lost. They offer a much smaller cut to the project in an area where they are already under budget and suggest several alternative cuts that can be made to other projects.

It can be tempting to second guess the decision or default to ad hoc decision-making when the impacts are no longer theoretical. However, it is important that the museum sticks to the resource allocation decision when faced with the scenario in the real world. Diverting from the resource allocation decision undercuts the value of the scenario planning process. It sends a signal to offices that they do not need to worry about being bound by these supposed decisions. To that end, if the decisions are not adhered to, perhaps it is not even worth offices meaningfully engaging in resource allocation planning. The real advocacy for their programs and projects can be reserved for when the crisis materializes.

The most important reason why the museum should not rethink its resource allocation decision is speed. Museum leaders are slowing their response to the very real challenge they currently face. The scenario planning process is intended to lower the stakes of difficult decisions by making them before a time of crisis. Questioning the process not only undercuts this decision support benefit but risks a worse outcome—total decision paralysis. The lack of discipline sends a message that disorganization rules the institution rather than advanced planning and informed action.

Adapting Resource Allocation Decisions

The example above was centered on museum leaders hesitating in a decision because it would be painful to carry out. This cautionary tale should not be taken to the extreme to imply that institutions must robotically abide by scenario planning regardless of the facts.

Not every scenario will be an exact fit for the real-world circumstances an institution may face. Consider our example of the museum that planned for a 5 percent budget decrease scenario. As the budget year is progressing, the museum is now projecting that revenue will be about 4 percent short of expectations.

The museum has a 5 percent resource allocation decision on the shelf ready to be implemented, so it may choose to implement the full decision to ensure it is secure if the projected revenue shortfall worsens throughout the year. This may be the selected approach if, for example, the original decision was to eliminate an entire project to achieve the desired savings. It may be impractical to remove nearly all of a project's resources and expect it to continue to limp along on the remainder.

Alternatively, the museum could use the 5 percent scenario as a starting point for the 4 percent need. The budget cuts outlined in the decision can serve as a menu of options from which to select a lesser set of actions. If the 5 percent decision involved across the board cuts to all offices, the museum can just cut a smaller percent. If the decision made targeted cuts to, say, five projects, the museum may only need to cut four of them.

The approach to this decision should revisit the same considerations originally used in scenario planning, such as impact to the strategic plan. Even with the time taken to revise the decision to align with the current circumstances, the museum's decision process will be more efficient than starting from scratch. Treating the resource allocation decision as a template for new decisions allows the museum to narrow its focus and move more quickly to address the challenge.

Consider if the museum with the 5 percent scenario faced a different reality: the revenue need is 8 percent. Perhaps this time it is not a revenue shortfall but an unanticipated world event or groundbreaking discovery that suddenly shifts the museum's priorities. The museum director is facing pressure from the museum's board to begin a new line of work, amounting to 8 percent of the current budget. Fundraising for the new project is getting underway, but existing funds need to be diverted from other areas to allow this project to begin right away.

The mandate to identify 8 percent in expense savings may be a shock to a museum that hasn't undergone scenario planning. But this museum is better able to adapt because it has already imagined what it would be like if the 5 percent scenario occurred. The simplest approach would be to begin by making all the cuts called for in the 5 percent decision. Of course, real-world events can happen at any time; they don't follow a budget cycle calendar.

The new priority may have arisen 3 months into the budget year. Activities that make up the 5 percent cut scenario have already incurred expenses. Now the progress toward the 8 percent goal is less than anticipated. Luckily, budget governance still has other resource allocation plans that were not originally included in the resource allocation decision. These plans provide a ready-made list of potential cuts to consider to reach the full need. Referencing these materials enables the museum to better meet the spirit of the budget as a living document when its needs change.

After all this talk of budget cuts, let us not forget how scenario planning can also position an institution to quickly act on funding opportunities. The decision to fund a project if the museum benefits from a 5 percent budget increase is most effective when carried through to other planning processes within the museum. This project should already align with the strategic plan, which helped budget governance identify it as the next highest priority for funding. The project owner should also ensure that the implementation plan is detailed and up-to-date so the project is ready for action if additional funding arrives. The project owner can also work with the development office to prepare a proposal for prospective donors so the funding scenario is more likely to become a reality.

FIRM CONNECTIONS

Scenario planning is not intended to be a prediction of a precise future but rather plausible and potential solutions about how to manage future decision-making. Much of an institution's ability to apply resource allocation decisions rests on its observations of changes in its environment. Not all scenarios come to fruition in a moment, like our earlier example of a grant being discontinued. They may be the accumulation of something happening—or not happening—over a period of time.

Strong strategic plan implementation and budget execution enable a museum to monitor internal factors that could trigger a budget scenario. Perhaps a project is falling behind schedule and leaving budget dollars on the table. The project's implementation plan should put the museum on alert that this strategic plan priority is missing its milestones. The museum may make the decision to apply extra effort to get the project back on track. The finance office may be able to identify how much budgeted funds will be underspent, providing budget governance with an opportunity to reallocate funds to the next priority for an increased funding scenario.

Resilience practices can provide early warning of an external scenario coming to fruition. If a scenario was built around a known risk, the museum can use KRIs to monitor the risk. Financial tools can project expected revenue and identify when actual revenue begins to exceed or fall short of established targets.

Leveraging scenario planning to make financial decisions plays an important role in cultivating resilience under FIRM. Curiosity is fostered by this new way of thinking. Curious institutions can expand the realm of imagined futures and shrink the unimaginable remainder. When leaders begin contemplating different futures, they become more skilled at interpreting trends and signals and anticipating outcomes. They will be more likely to observe connections that trigger the familiar logic of a previously examined scenario.

Faster recognition and response capabilities convey advantages far beyond the initial thought exercise. Paired with the other building blocks of the Resilience pillar—risk management, financial tools, and multi-year budgeting—institutions that engage in scenario planning are better prepared and more stable when confronting an uncertain future.

Chapter 10

Multi-year Budgeting

RESILIENCE BUILDING BLOCK 4

Multi-year budgeting is the final building block of the Resilience pillar. This is the last of the FIRM building blocks because of the advanced level of financial literacy and capability needed to carry it out. Multi-year budgeting requires adaptation of the annual budgeting process to an extended time horizon that asks budget owners to think well into the future. Financial tools and scenario planning can help an institution project future year resources. Strategic planning and risk management can guide budget owners in developing long-term spending plans. Governance and change management enable leaders to make informed decisions and engrain complex planning into institutional culture. This chapter explores how the connections established across all the building blocks of FIRM position a museum to take on the complex and difficult task of planning for its future.

Multi-year budgeting is a financial planning and management approach where budgets are prepared and planned for a period exceeding one budget year. The advantage of this approach is that it leverages all the financial information from the museum's systems and couples it with decisions about the institution's future. By planning beyond the typical one-year cycle, a museum can gain a long-term perspective on its financial trajectory.

Multi-year budgeting serves as the pivot point for the institution, by providing a financial roadmap for an extended period. Multi-year budgeting makes an institution more resilient by allowing the museum to anticipate and prepare for potential changes, disruptions, economic fluctuations, or new priorities that may unfold over several years.

Multi-year budgeting is increasingly being used in the public sector in different formats.[1] For instance, the city of Novi, Michigan, is required by state law to operate under an annual budget.[2] However, the city develops a three-year financial plan that it submits alongside its annual budget to highlight programs and priorities that will last beyond the annual budget period.[3] This approach allows the city to meet the state's annual budgeting requirements and prepare and present to the public a multi-year plan.

Lethbridge, Alberta, has tied its multi-year approach to the terms of local elected officials.[4] Newly elected officials can better understand what could be accomplished during their tenure, and budgets that cross between terms are less likely to be upended by political turmoil. The city of Calgary, Alberta, has found that the practice of multi-year budgeting has made it easier to secure government funding for long-term projects.[5]

The multi-year plan is not about tracking and accounting for every future dollar. That would be overwhelming and impossible to predict. It's about proactively managing the future of the museum's finances based on currently available information. Nor does it necessarily replace an annual budget cycle. The multi-year budget sets parameters and adds context to the one-year view. It makes the annual budget part of a larger plan with an eye toward the future. A museum can tailor its multi-year approach to its institutional governance and charter.

LONG-TERM FINANCIAL PLANNING

Major expenses and liabilities with a long-term impact benefit greatly from multi-year budgeting. Consider a museum that may have a loan with a balloon payment that will be coming due in three years. A museum with an annual budget would not consider this significant expenditure until the formulation period, perhaps only a year before the payment is due. The museum may be so focused on updating its steady annual costs that the anomalous balloon payment fails to be budgeted and comes as a surprise the year it is due. A multi-year budget will give the museum the opportunity to reserve the funds for this payment in its financial plan.

Most strategic initiatives require a commitment of resources that extend past one year. However, the owners of these initiatives may feel that they are limited in their ability to think strategically in an annual budget process. Segmenting a project into a single budget year may seem counterintuitive to all the long-term work they have done during implementation planning.

Multi-year budgeting enables an institution to draw a through line from its strategic plan to implementation planning to resource planning. When budget governance approves a multi-year budget, project owners know they have the long-term financial commitment of leadership. Without a multi-year budget, the museum may not fully achieve its strategic objectives because it is funding initiatives in fits and starts.

A museum with a large infrastructure project, like the replacement of its roof, would benefit from this approach. A project of this nature will be very expensive and may take well over five years to complete. Architects and engineers will be brought in to design the project. After that a construction firm will be hired to complete the project. The costs during the different phases of the project can be incorporated into the museum's multi-year budget to anticipate these funding needs. As the project progresses, and perhaps there are delays and cost overruns, the museum can update its multi-year budget to understand how these changes impact its financial position going forward.

Multi-year budgeting not only helps plan for long-term expenses but the long-term use of revenue as well. Imagine a museum receives a $50-million gift from a major donor. The donor does not provide the funds all at once, but $10 million a year over a five-year pledge schedule. Without any restrictions put in place by the donor, the funds can be used to support any museum needs. A museum that budgets annually will assume that the first $10 million received in year one is available as a projected source in its budget formulation. The museum may choose to fully utilize the source by assigning $10 million in uses for the budget year. This process repeats for five years until the $50 million is depleted.

Instead, perhaps this museum uses multi-year budgeting to plan its use of the $50 million. Rather than using a consistent $10 million a year as the funds become available, the museum can plan its use of the $50 million around its long-term needs. The museum may choose to use the funds to accomplish a new multi-year project—perhaps a project that scenario

Table 10.1 Budgeting Based on Pledge Schedule

	Year 1	*Year 2*	*Year 3*	*Year 4*	*Year 5*
$50m Gift	$10m	$10m	$10m	$10m	$10m

Source: Ashley Amos.

Table 10.2 Budgeting Based on Project Plan

	Year 1	*Year 2*	*Year 3*	*Year 4*	*Year 5*
$50m Gift	$7m	$9m	$13m	$15m	$6m

Source: Ashley Amos.

Table 10.3 Budgeting Based on Source Needs

	Year 1	*Year 2*	*Year 3*	*Year 4*	*Year 5*	*Year 6*
Expiring grant	$10m	$10m	$10m	$0	$0	$0
$50m Gift	$5m	$5m	$5m	$15m	$15m	$5m

Source: Ashley Amos.

planning identified as the next strategic priority should additional funding become available. The project's multi-year plan will outline variable funding needs throughout the different phases of the project.

Alternatively, the multi-year budget may consider this source in relation to the long-term projections for other sources. If a grant is expected to end in year three of the budget, the museum may use less of the $50 million in years one and two so that more of the gift remains available to support the museum in the years that follow. Regardless of the approach, multi-year budgeting allows the museum to place this $50 million gift into a larger context, which enables more informed decisions about when and how it is spent.

ENHANCING FUNDRAISING CONNECTIONS

The first chapter of this book highlighted the disconnect between the financial, fundraising, and programmatic functions of museums. Programs are carrying out projects and ongoing activities. Fundraisers are communicating with potential donors to secure general or specific support for museum work. The finance office is preparing annual budgets based on the information about projected sources, prepared in consultation with the development office, and planned uses, prepared by museum offices. These finance, fundraising, and program activities become more integrated as budgeting and strategic planning processes advance the museum toward a shared set of priorities.

Multi-year budgeting is one of the most significant steps a museum can take to further elevate these connections. A one-year budget will always be limited in its ability to synchronize with projects that take years to complete or with the long tail of fundraising campaigns and pledges. Expanding the budget view to multiple years places it more in line with the reality of fundraising and project timelines.

Let us return to our example of a $50 million unrestricted gift that has been pledged over the next five years. In the upcoming annual budget formulation, the museum will outline how to use the first $10 million to be received in that year. Without a programmatic area to which

Figure 10.1 Disjointed (Top) and Collaborative (Bottom) Mission Execution. *Source*: Ashley Amos.

this funding is restricted, the budget may assign the first $10 million to an array of activities in year one, the next $10 million to another set of activities in year two, and so on. The activities supported in each budget year may or may not be related. With disparate budgeting exercises carried out over the five-year pledge schedule, the museum may have a difficult time demonstrating to the donor the difference their support made.

If the museum instead utilizes a five-year budgeting approach, it can plan the uses for all the pledge payments from the start. The museum is positioned to tell the donor a clear story about successive years of work contributing toward larger goals. Revising and updating this plan each year, the museum will be more conscious of how diverting some of this funding to other work would disrupt the multi-year plan.

This example prompts the question of whether a savvy donor would have entered into an agreement for such a large amount without an understanding of what the museum planned to accomplish with the funds. The museum would likely be expected to provide the donor with a multi-year plan for the $50 million before the commitment was made. A museum that does not engage in multi-year budgeting will need to quickly estimate its future needs to prepare such a plan.

The same holds true if our example was a $50 million gift restricted to a specific high-profile project. The donor will expect the museum to provide a plan that demonstrates how their gift will advance or accomplish the project. The fundraising team will need to work with the project lead to build a multi-year view of planned project expenses. However, the existence of such a plan does not guarantee that it will be followed once the funds are received. There is a significant risk that the plan provided to the donor remains disconnected from the museum's budgeting process.

The finance, development, and program teams would have to revisit this plan each year to ensure the upcoming annual budget is formulated to align with donor expectations. Too often this follow-on action does not occur. Without continual monitoring, annual budgets may not assign the funds to the same work described in the multi-year plan. The annual spending reports sent to the donor will begin to diverge from what was promised. If the $50 million carries formal restrictions on its use, the museum risks violating the donor agreement. Even in our unrestricted example, the museum risks significant damage to the relationship with the donor.

If this institution moves to a holistic multi-year budgeting approach, the work already done on the long-term plans for large projects or specific gifts can serve as a starting point for a museum-wide multi-year budget. In the same year that a multi-year plan is prepared for a donor, this information can be added to the multi-year budget. The multi-year budget now ensures that what was communicated to the donor is formally incorporated into the museum's budgeting process. Each year that the multi-year budget is updated and a new annual budget is formulated, the museum can track if the plan is beginning to change. This change can be communicated back to the donor at the earliest opportunity so they are not surprised when spending reports are due.

The multi-year budget provides fundraising benefits that extend beyond this small set of high-profile projects and gifts. Without multi-year budgeting, it would require substantial resources for the fundraising office to work with each office in the museum to prepare fundraising proposals for everything they do. Because multi-year budgeting requires long-term costs for the entire museum, it creates data about numerous areas of work that may not previously have been targeted for donor proposals. The fundraising office now has a new repository of information that can be scaled to gifts of various size and purpose.

THE MULTI-YEAR BUDGET CYCLE

The actions needed to embark on multi-year budgeting will seem familiar to a museum with a robust annual budget process. Like annual budgeting, multi-year budgeting is structured within a budget cycle.

Budget Timeline

The first decision to make is the duration of the multi-year budget cycle. Multi-year budgets generally range from two to five years. The projections that will drive this long-term view are most useful if they cover a time period short enough to be predicted with some confidence, but long enough to reveal emerging shortfalls or other potential problems several years out.

A museum may have internal or external reasons that make moving away from an annual budget beneficial. Perhaps a museum receives government funds on a two-year cycle, but maintains the privately funded portion of its budget on a one-year cycle. Transitioning the entire budget to a two-year schedule allows the museum to bring its complex sources into alignment.

A museum's decision to begin multi-year budgeting may be tied to the appointment of a new museum director or the launch of a new strategic plan. This museum decides to establish

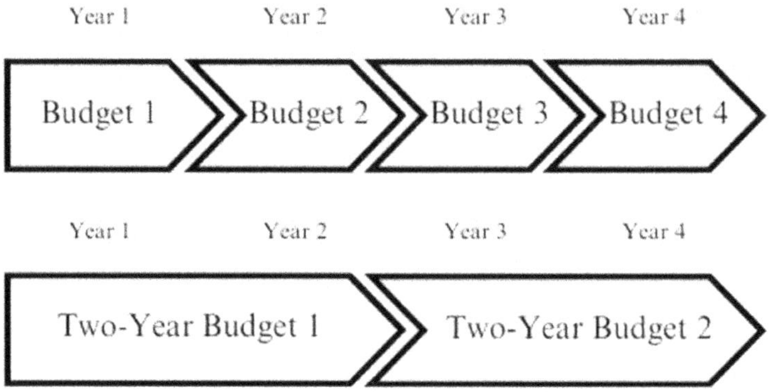

Figure 10.2 Two-Year Budget Timeline. *Source*: Ashley Amos.

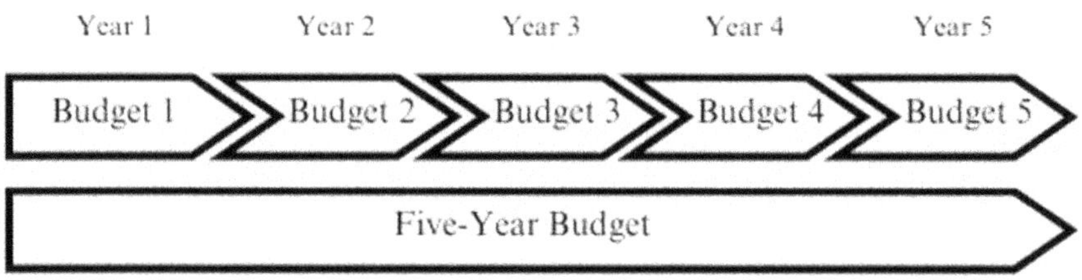

Figure 10.3 Five-Year Budget Timeline. *Source*: Ashley Amos.

a multi-year budget with a duration of five years—the same as its strategic plan. The museum continues to require an annual budget, perhaps due legislation, its charter, or the direction of the museum board. In this case, the annual budget is not being replaced; it is formulated alongside the broader multi-year plan. Together, these two budgets enable the museum to manage daily operations while keeping the long-term strategic direction of the institution in view.

Like all change, the implementation of multi-year budgeting need not happen all at once. Change management can apply an incremental approach. A museum that strives for a five-year budget timeline may begin by guiding offices through the creation of a two-year plan. As employees understand their role and value of longer-term planning, financial literacy will enable multi-year budgeting to become more advanced. The museum can gradually expand to three-, four-, and five-year budgeting over the course of several years.

Budget Formulation Guidance

As with annual budgeting, the multi-year budget cycle begins with the finance office preparing budget formulation guidance. The application of change management principles to a new multi-year budgeting effort requires the finance office to adapt budget guidance to what budget drafters are reasonably capable of.

As the institution acclimates to the multi-year budget cycle, growing financial literacy gradually improves the ability of budget drafters to make these future year expense estimates. Staff may independently begin to input more sophisticated future year estimates as they get more comfortable with multi-year budgeting. The finance office can monitor and build on this progress by increasing the expectations laid out by budget guidance in future budget cycles.

Projected Sources

Budget guidance is grounded in the museum's expectation of the revenue that will be available during the budget period. These are the sources that will later be paired with uses to form a spending plan. Finance can conduct an analysis of historical data to understand revenue trends. A review of pledge payment schedules can provide some indication of projected revenue, but these known payments may end sooner than the duration of the multi-year budget. Coordination with the development office to understand future year goals can fill out more of the assumption about projected available sources.

Multiple complex revenue streams will be more difficult to individually project in year five of a multi-year budget than they are in year one. Admission fees may be a reliable revenue stream that a museum can project based on historical trends alone, but major gifts from individual donors may be less consistent. The longer the budget period, the more finance will need to shift from specific funding projections by source to broader assumptions about revenue in a hypothetical future environment.

Financial tools can help by combining historical data, short-term projected revenue, and potential economic futures that can impact factors like endowment payouts and giving. A museum with robust strategic planning and risk management processes can also draw from those assessments of its internal and external environment to sharpen its future predictions.

Financial models can deliver a range of potential futures from which the finance office can choose. Finance may choose a steady assumption, expecting that revenue will follow the same trend line it has in recent years. Finance may instead choose a path of increased revenue, perhaps modeled on the assumption that a new fundraising campaign will begin next year. Economic conditions may prompt the finance office to plan for a decrease in revenue. If the institution is monitoring areas of high financial risk, it may be prudent to plan for austerity. The path selected will inform the budget guidance provided to offices as sources.

Projected Uses

The budget guidance also needs to set expectations as to how offices should estimate the expenses, or uses, they will be assigning to these sources. Budget drafters should by now be well equipped to prepare expense estimates through their experience with annual budgeting, but asking them to look further into the future may feel like new territory.

To help navigate this change, the museum can reinforce the connection to the implementation planning already underway in support of its strategic plan. Implementation plans provide a high-level view of when major projects should start, stop, or continue over the life of the strategic plan. This information can help orient an office to what it already knows about its future workload and become a starting point for quantifying the personnel and funding needed to support that work.

Some of the planned expenses will be based on personnel or contracts that are currently in place. These ongoing costs may be a significant portion of the multi-year budget, but will inflate each year. Personnel get pay raises, and contract costs may be subject to market rates. Budget guidance can provide standardized assumptions for these increases, such as a 3 percent annual cost inflation.

If a five-year lease agreement has built-in annual cost escalations, the office can input this more precise information rather than the standard assumption. Additional complexity can be added to the calculation of personnel costs, such as the impact of collective bargaining agreements or assumptions about the savings derived from vacant positions.

Not all expenses are going to remain steady with simple inflation over multiple years. Investment in a strategic priority may begin in year two of the budget, requiring new staff and contractual services. The current travel budget may be reduced in year three because the partnership with an overseas institution concludes. IT expenses may jump in year four when the museum's wireless internet system is due for an upgrade. Multi-year budgeting helps museums consider these annual variations far in advance so they are not caught off guard when it is time to think about the next budget year.

Multi-year budgeting is also helpful to an institution carrying out risk management. The museum has already spent significant time and resources planning for risks and determining risk management strategies. These strategies can now be incorporated into the multi-year budget to ensure appropriate resources are being applied across the time horizon of the risk.

Budget guidance must be clear about the level of detail expected for planned expenses. Naturally, the longer the budget period, the more difficult it would be to list and quantify specific budget lines at the same level as an annual budget.

A museum transitioning from a one-year to a two-year budget cycle may be able to project expenses with little change to the detail. Many expenses will be ongoing across the two years so they will not be difficult to maintain with an inflationary increase in year two. Several lines of work may start or stop in year two. The projects that are ending can estimate whether expenses trail off gradually or end at a planned date, but the resource needs of the new projects may be difficult to detail this early.

These challenges are magnified when taking on a multi-year budget as long as five years. A museum building a five-year budget should not expect offices to provide the same level of detail as they would to build five annual budgets. Multi-year budgets are meant to be summary documents, sketching a roadmap of the future rather than trying to describe every pebble that will be encountered along that road.

Planned expenses can be rolled up to a higher level with round numbers for cost estimates. Finance may reasonably expect that an office undertakes market research before estimating the cost of a new contract in the annual budget. However, if this contract is in year four of a multi-year budget, a much less precise (and less labor-intensive) figure will suffice as a placeholder.

Resource Prioritization

Regardless of how precise the cost estimate is, the true value of multi-year budgeting lies in learning how quickly the planned expenses catch up to projected sources. A museum can now view an array of planned expenses in future budget years to judge whether it is feasible to accomplish all its initiatives at once.

Perhaps an office is beginning a project in year four that requires a $3-million contract and 15 current staff. The office cannot also expect to continue using the same resources for another ongoing project. This is how multi-year budgeting can be a valuable planning tool. The office now has several years' notice to consider whether the ongoing project can be completed in year three to free up the needed resources or if the new project should be delayed until year five.

The effects of these trade-offs extend beyond the budget process. The exercise of resourcing future projects provides an additional layer of rigor to implementation plans. Strategic planning governance will want to know if starting the project in year four does not appear realistic. They must make the decision of whether to update the implementation plan to delay the project or prepare a resource allocation plan that proposes this project for a budget increase scenario.

Multi-year budgeting can help a museum right-size its budget by building plans to address areas of underperformance. Let's say that historical data shows that year after year an office spends only 60 percent of its budget. The rest of the museum averages a 90 percent budget execution rate. This office has a $5 million budget, but generally spends only $3 million. Because the museum builds each budget based on the prior year's budget, the office continues to receive $5 million plus inflation each year.

The office is taking up valuable sources in the budget that could be used to support other initiatives. Worse still, the office's implementation planning milestones are repeatedly pushed into the future when they cannot be met. Slow spending and project delays indicate that the office is biting off more than it can chew, and it lacks the capacity to carry out all the work it wants to take on.

Annual budgeting can certainly respond to poor budget execution by reducing the amount allocated to that office in the next budget formulation guidance. However, cutting a $5m office to $3m in an annual budgeting process may seem drastic and cause morale to plummet. Multi-year budgeting provides an opportunity to set this office on a sustainable path. Perhaps the office's budget is baselined at $3 million in year one of the multi-year budget with standard inflation assumptions applied in the out-years. Strategic planning governance works with the office to prioritize the use of the $3 million to support its highest-priority projects. Other projects that are distracting from these priorities are closed out or paused.

The budget also establishes a multi-year plan for building the office's capacity. In year one, employees who were previously working on other projects are added to the priority projects. The budget plans for incremental investments each year—a new project manager in year one and a support contract in year two. As capacity increases, year three of the budget adds the next strategic priority project to the office's workload along with additional funding to carry it out. The implementation plan for each project is updated to reflect this multi-year timeline.

A five-year budget that adds inflation, capacity investments, and project expansion may actually result in a higher budget than the $5 million the office started with. But now, the office is positioned to actually spend its funds and carry out its work on schedule. The use of multi-year budgeting in this case allows the museum to take a longer view of the office's future. The budget demonstrates that the office is not just being cut but placed on an achievable growth path that will make it more successful in the long run. This path can then be monitored in future years to see if budget execution improves and project timelines are met. In the meantime, the museum can redeploy the funds removed from this office's budget each year to support other resource priorities across the institution.

Budget Approval

Approval of the draft multi-year budget follows the same path established for annual budgeting. The finance office works with offices to validate their spending plans and ensure that sources and uses balance. The assembled budget is reviewed by budget governance, which coordinates with strategic planning governance. This step is even more valuable than in annual budgeting because the multi-year budget provides a broader view of the institution's intended progress toward its long-term goals. Viewing implementation plans against resource availability may raise concerns as to whether the budget is getting out of step with strategic priorities.

Scenario planning on a multi-year scale can help governance think outside the bounds of the projected available sources. Governance can make decisions about potential budget increase and decrease scenarios that may allow them to speed—or force them to slow—areas of work in future years. These resource allocation decisions will prove to be valuable planning tools when the anticipated sources for a future year inevitably vary from the budget assumption.

Budget Execution

The mantra that a budget is just a plan continues to apply when multi-year budgets enter the budget execution phase. We have already explored how a regular revision schedule helps an institution adapt annual budgets to changing circumstances throughout the budget year. Multi-year budgeting provides even more time for the plan to become outdated.

Recall our museum that is moving from an annual to a two-year budget. The museum may keep the same revision schedule currently used for its annual budget or it may reduce the revision frequency only slightly. If the museum revised its annual budget monthly, it may move to a quarterly schedule. If the budget was revised quarterly, the museum may shift to biannual updates.

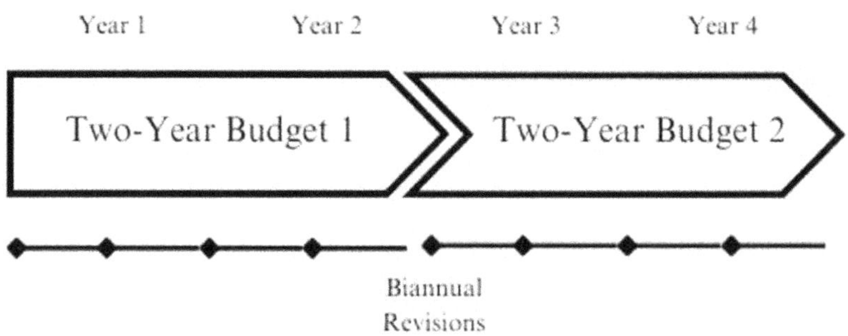

Figure 10.4 Two-Year Budget Revision Schedule. *Source*: Ashley Amos.

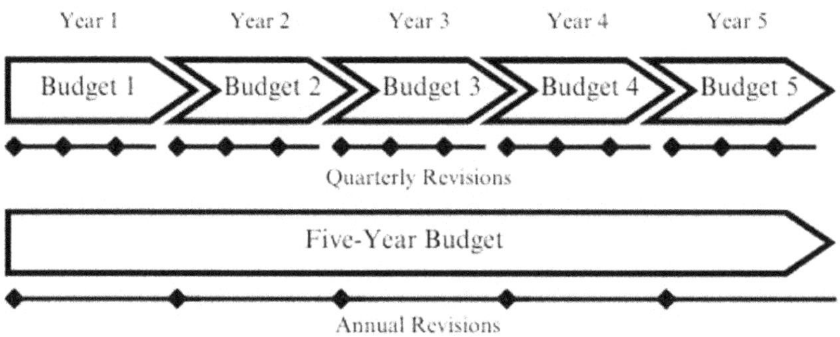

Figure 10.5 Five-Year Budget Revision Schedule. *Source*: Ashley Amos.

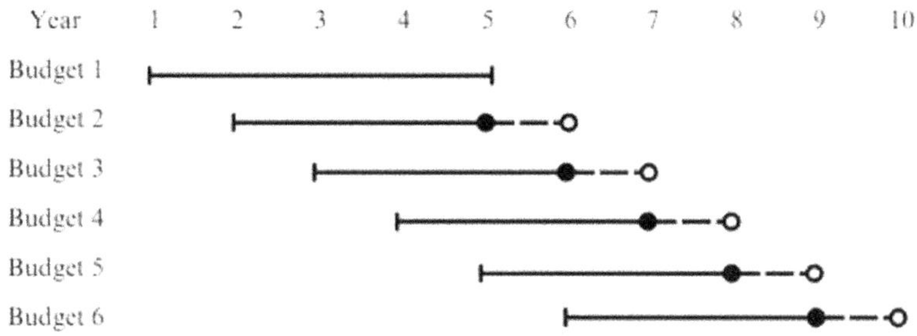

Figure 10.6 Overlapping Multi-Year Budget Timelines. *Source*: Ashley Amos.

Consider instead the museum that is beginning five-year budgeting as a supplement to its annual budget. This museum will continue to revise its annual budget on its regular quarterly schedule. The first year of the five-year budget is the same as the annual budget, so the museum may wonder if it needs to keep the two in lockstep.

Imagine the cost of a contract turns out to be higher than an office budgeted. The office updates the annual budget to reflect this new information and reduces spending in another area to offset the increase. However, year one of the five-year budget does not need to be revised to mirror the annual budget. The annual budget is the detailed plan that is being executed in real time. There are far too many budget changes throughout the year to keep up with revising two budgets in tandem.

Instead, the five-year budget is revised annually during budget formulation season. Year one of the five-year budget has now been completed so it is removed from the budget and a new year of estimated sources and uses is added to the end. The assumptions of the next four years are updated to reflect any new information learned in the last budget year.

The office in our example may not only face an increased contract cost in this budget year but also expects the higher cost to continue or even escalate throughout the life of the project. The office will use this information to update its estimated project costs in the five-year budget revision.

Museum-wide adjustments to the budget may be necessary during multi-year budget revision. Perhaps during the last budget year, the cost of employee benefits jumped three percent. The previously prepared multi-year budget assumed a steady one percent increase each year. In revising the multi-year personnel cost assumptions, the museum will establish the prior year actual cost of benefits as the starting point and reassess whether the annual inflation should be higher than one percent in future years.

As these examples demonstrate, the first exercise in multi-year budgeting is the most difficult. Offices start with a blank page and are asked to populate every year of the multi-year budget. Once a museum makes it through this big lift, the future years are focused primarily on making adjustments and adding a new year to the end of the timeline.

FIRM CONNECTIONS

As referenced throughout this book, the building blocks of FIRM can be implemented incrementally and concurrently; each block does not need to be fully realized before starting the next. However, standing up a multi-year budgeting capability is less daunting when an institution has made at least some progress across the other building blocks. When implemented this way, a multi-year budget can serve as the capstone to FIRM. Financial literacy, budgeting, strategic planning, governance, change management, risk management, financial tools, and scenario planning all come together to support an institution's ability to plan for its future through multi-year budgeting.

Part V

THE FUTURE OF FINANCIAL MANAGEMENT

Chapter 11

Connecting the Financial Ecosystem

Now that we have explored each of FIRM's eight building blocks, it is important to revisit the self-assessment from chapter 1. Readers should compare the two versions of their completed assessment to see if their understanding of their institution's current state has evolved from their initial evaluation. For instance, some capabilities that were previously rated as "advanced" may be reassessed as "intermediate" because they lack connections to the broader financial ecosystem.

The updated self-assessment is a tool that readers can use to form a plan for targeted progress in their office or institution. Consider opportunities to establish individual capabilities that are lacking and build connections between existing capabilities. Target areas can be advanced by applying the financial literacy techniques of documentation, standardization, simplification, and modernization.

The eight building blocks are not expected to be put in place overnight. FIRM requires a sustained and collective effort by museum leadership to prioritize financial health and stability as an essential part of museum culture. FIRM asks a lot of museum leaders—investing their time, money, and political capital to establish new ways of doing business. The strength of the model lies in the mutual support each building block provides to the others. Adopting one or more of the building blocks of FIRM will advance an institution, but only by assembling the building blocks together can the solid structure of an integrated and resilient museum be fully realized.

New ways of thinking enhance connections between short-term operations and long-term goals. Employees are equipped with the financial knowledge, role clarity, and tools to help them advance the institution from the bottom up. Supportive processes and decision structures pair with a capacity for change to help a museum move its many parts as one. Preparing and planning for potential futures that can alter a museum's path help regain control of an institution's environment. The connections established through FIRM enable a museum to maximize the benefits of each capability and build a culture that will continue to promote sound financial management long into the future.

We hope that the pillars and building blocks of FIRM, distilled from decades of best practices, will provide museums with the financial health and stability to weather economic uncertainty. The FIRM self-assessment should be revisited over time to chart advancements as they are made and highlight any ongoing areas of weakness. If museum leaders steadily advance the principles we have outlined, their institutions will be in the best position possible to continue carrying out their missions and serving their communities for many years to come.

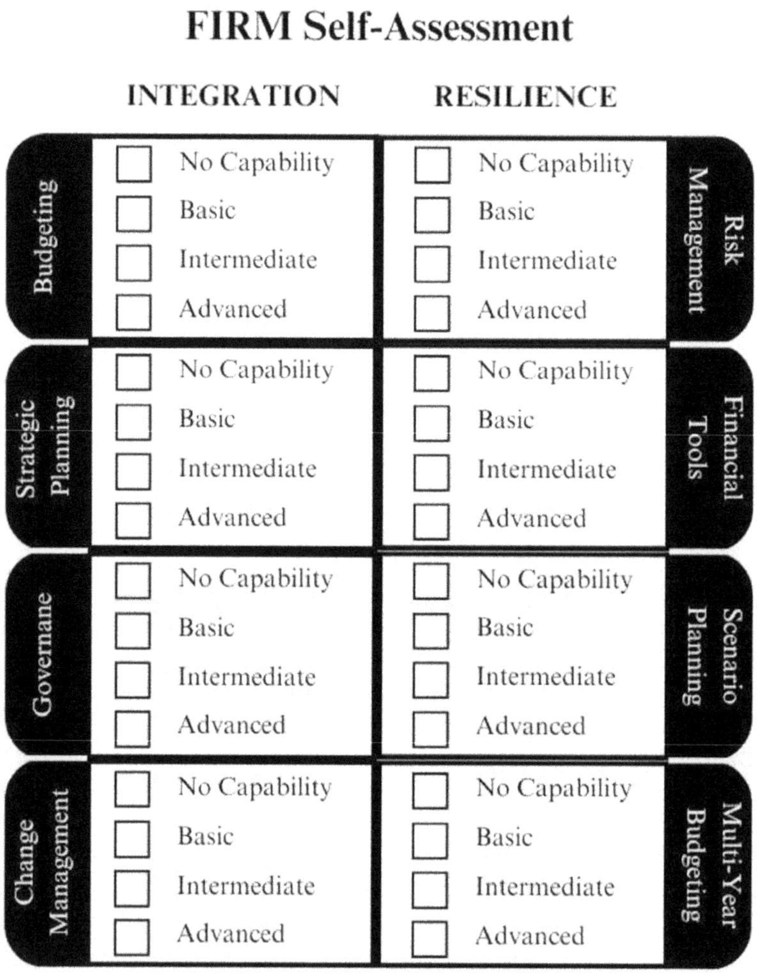

Figure 11.1 Self-assessment. *Source*: Ashley Amos.

Notes

CHAPTER 1

1. Office of the Surgeon General. 2023. "Our Epidemic of Loneliness and Isolation: The Surgeon General's Advisory on the Healing Effects of Social Connection and Community." HHS.gov. https://www.hhs.gov/sites/default/files/surgeon-general-social-connection-advisory.pdf.

2. Office of the Surgeon General. 2023. "Our Epidemic of Loneliness and Isolation: The Surgeon General's Advisory on the Healing Effects of Social Connection and Community." HHS.gov. https://www.hhs.gov/sites/default/files/surgeon-general-social-connection-advisory.pdf.

3. American Alliance of Museums. 2021. "Museums and Trust." American Alliance of Museums. https://www.aam-us.org/wp-content/uploads/2021/09/Museums-and-Trust-2021.pdf.

4. BDO USA. 2023. "Nonprofit Standards: Benchmarking Survey." BDO. https://insights.bdo.com/rs/116-EDP-270/images/NPE_2023-Benchmarking_Report-OVERVIEW.pdf.

5. Culgan, Skena. 2024. "First look: See inside the Brooklyn Museum's new Toby Devan Lewis Education Center." TimeOut, January 19, 2024. https://www.timeout.com/newyork/news/the-brooklyn-museum-is-opening-a-completely-revamped-education-center-011924.

6. Culgan, Skena. 2024. "First look: See inside the Brooklyn Museum's new Toby Devan Lewis Education Center." TimeOut, January 19, 2024. https://www.timeout.com/newyork/news/the-brooklyn-museum-is-opening-a-completely-revamped-education-center-011924.

7. Small, Zachary. 2024. "Rubin Museum, Haven for Asian Art, to Close After 20 Years." *The New York Times*, February 6, 2024. https://www.nytimes.com/2024/01/31/arts/design/rubin-museum-closing.html?searchResultPosition=1.

8. Small, Zachary. 2024. "Rubin Museum, Haven for Asian Art, to Close After 20 Years." *The New York Times*, February 6, 2024. https://www.nytimes.com/2024/01/31/arts/design/rubin-museum-closing.html?searchResultPosition=1.

9. Tremayne-Pengelly, Alexandra. 2024. "The Met Just Sold a $2.8M George Washington Portrait to Fund Future Acquisitions." *Observer*, January 25, 2024. https://observer.com/2024/01/met-george-washington-portrait-acquisition-fund/.

10. American Alliance of Museums. 2021. "2021-AAM-Museum-Facts-Details-FINAL.pdf." American Alliance of Museums. https://www.aam-us.org/wp-content/uploads/2021/02/2021-AAM-Museum-Facts-Details-FINAL.pdf.

11. Smithsonian. 2023. "Smithsonian Fiscal Year 2023 Federal Budget Totals More Than $1 Billion." SI. https://www.si.edu/newsdesk/releases/smithsonian-fiscal-year-2023-federal-budget-totals-more-1-billion.

12. Haimerl, Amy. 2021. "What Keeps U.S. Art Museums Running—and How Might the Pandemic Change That?" *ARTnews*. https://www.artnews.com/art-news/news/united-states-art-museum-financing-1234584930/.

13. NYC Cultural Affairs. 2024. "History of Cultural Institutions Group." NYC Cultural Affairs. https://www.nyc.gov/site/dcla/cultural-funding/history-of-city-owned-cultural-institutions.page.

14. NYC Cultural Affairs. 2024. "History of Cultural Institutions Group." NYC Cultural Affairs. https://www.nyc.gov/site/dcla/cultural-funding/history-of-city-owned-cultural-institutions.page.

15. Velie, Elaine. 2024. "Museum Leaders Urge NYC Mayor to Reverse Budget Cuts." Hyperallergic. https://hyperallergic.com/866639/museum-leaders-urge-nyc-mayor-eric-adams-to-reverse-budget-cuts-dcla/.

16. American Alliance of Museums. 2024. "Museums Advocacy Day." American Alliance of Museums. https://www.aam-us.org/programs/museums-advocacy-day/.

17. American Alliance of Museums. 2024. "Museums Advocacy Day." American Alliance of Museums. https://www.aam-us.org/programs/museums-advocacy-day/.

18. American Alliance of Museums. n.d. "Advocate from Anywhere – American Alliance of Museums." American Alliance of Museums. Accessed March 9, 2024. https://www.aam-us.org/programs/advocacy/advocate-from-anywhere/.

19. NYC Cultural Affairs. 2024. "History of Cultural Institutions Group." NYC Cultural Affairs. https://www.nyc.gov/site/dcla/cultural-funding/history-of-city-owned-cultural-institutions.page.

20. Haimerl, Amy. 2021. "What Keeps U.S. Art Museums Running—and How Might the Pandemic Change That?" *ARTnews*. https://www.artnews.com/art-news/news/united-states-art-museum-financing-1234584930/.

21. Haimerl, Amy. 2021. "What Keeps U.S. Art Museums Running—and How Might the Pandemic Change That?" *ARTnews*. https://www.artnews.com/art-news/news/united-states-art-museum-financing-1234584930/.

22. Bellafante, Ginia. 2023. "Why Has This 258-Year-Old Mansion Been Left to Fall Apart?" *The New York Times*, October 27, 2023. https://www.nytimes.com/2023/10/27/nyregion/morris-jumel-mansion-renovation-repair.html.

23. Luscombe, Richard. 2024. "Ron DeSantis strips more than $32m in Florida arts funding." *The Guardian*, June 30, 2024. https://www.theguardian.com/us-news/article/2024/jun/30/ron-desantis-florida-art-funding-cut. Gebregiorgis, Senait. 2024. "Arts and culture funding cuts could impact jobs and education." WESH, July 11, 2024. https://www.wesh.com/article/arts-and-culture-funding-cuts-florida/61573348.

24. Florida Cultural Alliance. 2023. "2024-2025 Arts & Culture Funding Recommendations." flca.net. https://flca.net/wp-content/uploads/2023/12/2024-Platform-Book-12.15.23-1.pdf.

25. Detroit Institute of Arts. n.d. "Tri-County Benefits." Detroit Institute of Arts. Accessed July 25, 2024. https://dia.org/community/tri-county-benefits.

26. Marini, Miriam. 2022. "The DIA collects hundreds of millions from taxpayers. What do residents get back?" *Outlier Media*, November 17, 2022. https://outliermedia.org/dia-detroit-institute-of-arts-millage-wayne-county/.

27. Salort-Pons, Salvador. 2024. "A Model for Financial Stability at the Detroit Institute of Arts." The Wall Street Journal, February 14, 2024. https://www.wsj.com/articles/a-model-for-financial-stability-at-the-detroit-institute-of-arts-millage-196bfbcc.

28. Detroit Institute of Arts. n.d. "Tri-County Benefits." Detroit Institute of Arts. Accessed July 25, 2024. https://dia.org/community/tri-county-benefits.

29. Marini, Miriam. 2022. "The DIA collects hundreds of millions from taxpayers. What do residents get back?" *Outlier Media*, November 17, 2022. https://outliermedia.org/dia-detroit-institute-of-arts-millage-wayne-county/.

30. Raicovich, Laura, and Laura Hanna. 2024. "To Save Museums, Fund Them Like Highways." *The New York Times*, February 10, 2024. https://www.nytimes.com/2024/02/10/opinion/museums-funding-arts-infrastructure.html?searchResultPosition=1.

31. Giving USA. 2024. Giving USA 2023 Infographic, 2023 Summary of Giving USA Annual Report. Giving USA.

32. Giving USA. 2024. Giving USA 2023 Infographic, 2023 Summary of Giving USA Annual Report. Giving USA.

33. BDO USA. 2023. "Nonprofit Standards: Benchmarking Survey." BDO. https://insights.bdo.com/rs/116-EDP-270/images/NPE_2023-Benchmarking_Report-OVERVIEW.pdf.

34. Haimerl, Amy. 2021. "What Keeps U.S. Art Museums Running—and How Might the Pandemic Change That?" *ARTnews*. https://www.artnews.com/art-news/news/united-states-art-museum-financing-1234584930/.

35. BDO USA. 2023. "Nonprofit Standards: Benchmarking Survey." BDO. https://insights.bdo.com/rs/116-EDP-270/images/NPE_2023-Benchmarking_Report-OVERVIEW.pdf.

36. Schrader, Adam, Katie White, and Jo Lawson. 2024. "A Cyberattack Hits Software Used by Museums, Causing Online Collections to Go Down." *Artnet News*, January 4, 2024. https://news.artnet.com/art-world/cyberattack-hits-software-used-by-museums-online-collections-2416159.

37. Schrader, Adam, Katie White, and Jo Lawson. 2024. "A Cyberattack Hits Software Used by Museums, Causing Online Collections to Go Down." *Artnet News*, January 4, 2024. https://news.artnet.com/art-world/cyberattack-hits-software-used-by-museums-online-collections-2416159.

38. Gartner. 2023. "Gartner Forecasts Worldwide IT Spending to Grow 8% in 2024." Gartner. https://www.gartner.com/en/newsroom/press-releases/2023-10-18-gartner-forecasts-worldwide-it-spending-to-grow-8-percent-in-2024.

39. Anderson, Sonja. 2024. "Climate Activists Throw Soup at the 'Mona Lisa.'" *Smithsonian Magazine*. https://www.smithsonianmag.com/smart-news/climate-activists-throw-soup-mona-lisa-leonardo-da-vinci-180983677.

40. U.S. Holocaust Memorial Museum. 2024. "Stephen Tyrone Johns (1969–2009)." U.S. Holocaust Memorial Museum. https://www.ushmm.org/information/press/in-memoriam/stephen-tyrone-johns-1969-2009.

41. Marcelo, Philip. 2024. "Museum in NYC closing 2 halls of Native objects." *Arkansas Democrat-Gazette*, January 28, 2024. https://www.arkansasonline.com/news/2024/jan/28/museum-in-nyc-closing-2-halls-of-native-objects/.

42. Marcelo, Philip. 2024. "Museum in NYC closing 2 halls of Native objects." *Arkansas Democrat-Gazette*, January 28, 2024. https://www.arkansasonline.com/news/2024/jan/28/museum-in-nyc-closing-2-halls-of-native-objects/.

43. Small, Zachary. 2023. "Guggenheim Lays Off 10 Employees as Museums Face Fiscal Challenges." *The New York Times*, December 4, 2023. https://www.nytimes.com/2023/12/04/arts/design/guggenheim-museum-lay-offs.html.

44. Small, Zachary. 2023. "Guggenheim Lays Off 10 Employees as Museums Face Fiscal Challenges." *The New York Times*, December 4, 2023. https://www.nytimes.com/2023/12/04/arts/design/guggenheim-museum-lay-offs.html.

45. Small, Zachary. 2023. "Guggenheim Lays Off 10 Employees as Museums Face Fiscal Challenges." *The New York Times*, December 4, 2023. https://www.nytimes.com/2023/12/04/arts/design/guggenheim-museum-lay-offs.html.

46. Small, Zachary. 2023. "Guggenheim Lays Off 10 Employees as Museums Face Fiscal Challenges." *The New York Times*, December 4, 2023. https://www.nytimes.com/2023/12/04/arts/design/guggenheim-museum-lay-offs.html.

47. BDO USA. 2023. "Nonprofit Standards: Benchmarking Survey." BDO. https://insights.bdo.com/rs/116-EDP-270/images/NPE_2023-Benchmarking_Report-OVERVIEW.pdf.

48. Frank, Richard B. 2021. "The Three Missed Tactical Warnings That Could Have Made a Difference at Pearl Harbor." The National WWII Museum. https://www.nationalww2museum.org/war/articles/pearl-harbor-missed-tactical-warnings.

49. Frank, Richard B. 2021. "The Three Missed Tactical Warnings That Could Have Made a Difference at Pearl Harbor." The National WWII Museum. https://www.nationalww2museum.org/war/articles/pearl-harbor-missed-tactical-warnings.

CHAPTER 2

1. Nations Online. 2024. "Languages of the World A Nations Online Project." Nations Online. https://www.nationsonline.org/oneworld/languages.htm.

2. Vansynghel, Margo. 2024. "Bellevue Arts Museum faces 'dire' financial crisis." *Seattle Times*, February 16, 2024. https://www.seattletimes.com/entertainment/visual-arts/bellevue-arts-museum-faces-dire-financial-crisis/.

3. Vansynghel, Margo. 2024. "Bellevue Arts Museum faces 'dire' financial crisis." *Seattle Times*, February 16, 2024. https://www.seattletimes.com/entertainment/visual-arts/bellevue-arts-museum-faces-dire-financial-crisis/.

4. Vansynghel, Margo. 2024. "Bellevue Arts Museum faces 'dire' financial crisis." *Seattle Times*, February 16, 2024. https://www.seattletimes.com/entertainment/visual-arts/bellevue-arts-museum-faces-dire-financial-crisis/.

5. Strom, Stephanie. 2006. "A Struggle for Solvency at Milwaukee Museum." *The New York Times*, January 29, 2006. https://www.nytimes.com/2006/01/29/us/a-struggle-for-solvency-at-milwaukee-museum.html.

6. Strom, Stephanie. 2006. "A Struggle for Solvency at Milwaukee Museum." *The New York Times*, January 29, 2006. https://www.nytimes.com/2006/01/29/us/a-struggle-for-solvency-at-milwaukee-museum.html.

7. Strom, Stephanie. 2006. "A Struggle for Solvency at Milwaukee Museum." *The New York Times*, January 29, 2006. https://www.nytimes.com/2006/01/29/us/a-struggle-for-solvency-at-milwaukee-museum.html.

8. Spoto, Cara. 2024. "Milwaukee Public Museum has now raised $80 million in private donations for new museum." *Biz Times*, March 12, 2024. https://biztimes.com/milwaukee-public-museum-has-now-raised-80-million-in-private-donations-for-new-museum/.

9. Mullins, Luke. 2012. "Crisis at the Corcoran." *Washingtonian*, November 27, 2012. https://www.washingtonian.com/2012/11/27/crisis-at-the-corcoran/.

10. Mullins, Luke. 2012. "Crisis at the Corcoran." *Washingtonian*, November 27, 2012. https://www.washingtonian.com/2012/11/27/crisis-at-the-corcoran/.

11. Mullins, Luke. 2012. "Crisis at the Corcoran." *Washingtonian*, November 27, 2012. https://www.washingtonian.com/2012/11/27/crisis-at-the-corcoran/.

12. Note, Natalie, and Rachel Moon. 2024. "Students, faculty reflect on GW's acquisition of Corcoran, 10 years later." *The GW Hatchet*, March 6, 2024. https://gwhatchet.com/2024/03/04/students-faculty-reflect-on-gws-acquisition-of-corcoran-10-years-later/.

13. Note, Natalie, and Rachel Moon. 2024. "Students, faculty reflect on GW's acquisition of Corcoran, 10 years later." *The GW Hatchet*, March 6, 2024. https://gwhatchet.com/2024/03/04/students-faculty-reflect-on-gws-acquisition-of-corcoran-10-years-later/. Mullins, Luke. 2012. "Crisis at the Corcoran." *Washingtonian*, November 27, 2012. https://www.washingtonian.com/2012/11/27/crisis-at-the-corcoran/.

CHAPTER 3

1. Boehm, Mike. 2008. "L.A.'S MOCA IN DEEP FINANCIAL TROUBLE." *Los Angeles Times*, November 19, 2008. https://www.latimes.com/archives/la-xpm-2008-nov-19-et-moca19-story.html.

2. Boehm, Mike. 2008. "L.A.'S MOCA IN DEEP FINANCIAL TROUBLE." *Los Angeles Times*, November 19, 2008. https://www.latimes.com/archives/la-xpm-2008-nov-19-et-moca19-story.html.

3. Pogrebin, Robin. 2021. "Amid Signs of Trouble, Can MOCA Find Its Footing?." *The New York Times*, May 3, 2021. https://www.nytimes.com/2021/05/02/arts/design/Can-LA-MOCA-Regain-Footing.html.

4. Pogrebin, Robin. 2021. "Amid Signs of Trouble, Can MOCA Find Its Footing?." *The New York Times*, May 3, 2021. https://www.nytimes.com/2021/05/02/arts/design/Can-LA-MOCA-Regain-Footing.html.

5. 103rd US Congress. 1993. "PUBLIC LAW 103-62." Congress.gov. Accessed March 15, 2024. https://www.govinfo.gov/content/pkg/STATUTE-107/pdf/STATUTE-107-Pg285.pdf.

6. 103rd US Congress. 1993. "PUBLIC LAW 103-62." Congress.gov. Accessed March 15, 2024. https://www.govinfo.gov/content/pkg/STATUTE-107/pdf/STATUTE-107-Pg285.pdf.

CHAPTER 4

1. Nyarku, Kwamena, and Gloria Agyapong. 2011. "Rediscovering SWOT Analysis: The Extended Version." Academic Leadership: The Online Journal 9, no. 2 (April): Article 28.

2. Nyarku, Kwamena, and Gloria Agyapong. 2011. "Rediscovering SWOT Analysis: The Extended Version." Academic Leadership: The Online Journal 9, no. 2 (April): Article 28.

3. *Principles of Management*. 2015. N.p.: University of Minnesota Libraries Publishing. https://open.lib.umn.edu/principlesmanagement/chapter/4-3-the-roles-of-mission-vision-and-values/.

4. *Principles of Management*. 2015. N.p.: University of Minnesota Libraries Publishing. https://open.lib.umn.edu/principlesmanagement/chapter/4-3-the-roles-of-mission-vision-and-values/.

5. Haughey, Duncan. 2014. "A Brief History of SMART Goals." Project Smart. https://www.projectsmart.co.uk/smart-goals/brief-history-of-smart-goals.php.

6. Doran, George T. 1981. "There's a S.M.A.R.T. way to write management's goals and objectives." AMA Forum, (November). https://community.mis.temple.edu/mis0855002fall2015/files/2015/10/S.M.A.R.T-Way-Management-Review.pdf.

7. Haughey, Duncan. 2014. "A Brief History of SMART Goals." Project Smart. https://www.projectsmart.co.uk/smart-goals/brief-history-of-smart-goals.php.

CHAPTER 5

1. Project Management Institute. n.d. "What is Project Management, Approaches, and PMI." PMI. Accessed June 19, 2024. https://www.pmi.org/about/what-is-project-management.

CHAPTER 6

1. Ewenstein, Boris, Wesley Smith, and Ashvin Sologar. 2015. "Changing Change Management." McKinsey. https://www.mckinsey.com/featured-insights/leadership/changing-change-management.

2. Odor, Hillary O. 2018. "Organisational Change and Development." *European Journal of Business and Management* 10 (7): 58-66. ISSN 2222-2839.

3. Odor, Hillary O. 2018. "Organisational Change and Development." *European Journal of Business and Management* 10 (7): 58-66. ISSN 2222-2839.

4. Pope, John. 2021. "A War Story: The History of the National World War II Museum in New Orleans." *NOLA.com*, July 7, 2021. https://www.nola.com/300/article_8dadb6df-bcfe-56ce-ba8f-ff92c0551a8a.html.

5. Pope, John. 2021. "A War Story: The History of the National World War II Museum in New Orleans." *NOLA.com*, July 7, 2021. https://www.nola.com/300/article_8dadb6df-bcfe-56ce-ba8f-ff92c0551a8a.html.

6. Odor, Hillary O. 2018. "Organisational Change and Development." *European Journal of Business and Management* 10 (7): 58-66. ISSN 2222-2839.

7. Odor, Hillary O. 2018. "Organisational Change and Development." *European Journal of Business and Management* 10 (7): 58-66. ISSN 2222-2839.

8. Andersen, Erika. 2022. "Change Is Hard. Here's How to Make It Less Painful." *Harvard Business Review*. https://hbr.org/2022/04/change-is-hard-heres-how-to-make-it-less-painful.

9. Andersen, Erika. 2022. "Change Is Hard. Here's How to Make It Less Painful." *Harvard Business Review*. https://hbr.org/2022/04/change-is-hard-heres-how-to-make-it-less-painful.

10. Andersen, Erika. 2022. "Change Is Hard. Here's How to Make It Less Painful." *Harvard Business Review*. https://hbr.org/2022/04/change-is-hard-heres-how-to-make-it-less-painful.

11. Lewin, Kurt. 1947. "Frontiers in Group Dynamics: Concept, Method and Reality in Social Science; Social Equilibria and Social Change." *Human Relations* 1, no. 1 (June): 5-41. https://doi.org/10.1177/001872674700100103.

12. Lewin, Kurt. 1947. "Frontiers in Group Dynamics: Concept, Method and Reality in Social Science; Social Equilibria and Social Change." *Human Relations* 1, no. 1 (June): 5-41. https://doi.org/10.1177/001872674700100103.

13. Lewin, Kurt. 1947. "Frontiers in Group Dynamics: Concept, Method and Reality in Social Science; Social Equilibria and Social Change." Human Relations 1, no. 1 (June): 5-41. https://doi.org/10.1177/001872674700100103.

14. Lewin, Kurt. 1947. "Frontiers in Group Dynamics: Concept, Method and Reality in Social Science; Social Equilibria and Social Change." *Human Relations* 1, no. 1 (June): 5-41. https://doi.org/10.1177/001872674700100103.

15. Odor, Hillary O. 2018. "Organisational Change and Development." *European Journal of Business and Management* 10 (7): 58-66. ISSN 2222-2839.

16. Andersen, Erika. 2022. "Change Is Hard. Here's How to Make It Less Painful." *Harvard Business Review*. https://hbr.org/2022/04/change-is-hard-heres-how-to-make-it-less-painful.

17. Odor, Hillary O. 2018. "Organisational Change and Development." *European Journal of Business and Management* 10 (7): 58-66. ISSN 2222-2839.

18. Andersen, Erika. 2022. "Change Is Hard. Here's How to Make It Less Painful." *Harvard Business Review*. https://hbr.org/2022/04/change-is-hard-heres-how-to-make-it-less-painful.

19. Odor, Hillary O. 2018. "Organisational Change and Development." *European Journal of Business and Management* 10 (7): 58-66. ISSN 2222-2839.

CHAPTER 7

1. Morris, Gregory D. 2018. "A Brief History of Marine Insurance." Risk & Insurance. https://riskandinsurance.com/brief-history-marine-insurance/.

2. Morris, Gregory D. 2018. "A Brief History of Marine Insurance." Risk & Insurance. https://riskandinsurance.com/brief-history-marine-insurance/.

3. Morris, Gregory D. 2018. "A Brief History of Marine Insurance." Risk & Insurance. https://riskandinsurance.com/brief-history-marine-insurance/.

4. Isaacson, Walter. 2003. *Benjamin Franklin: An American Life*. N.p.: Simon & Schuster.

5. Isaacson, Walter. 2003. *Benjamin Franklin: An American Life*. N.p.: Simon & Schuster.

6. Isaacson, Walter. 2003. *Benjamin Franklin: An American Life*. N.p.: Simon & Schuster.

7. Richardson, Gary, Alejandro Komai, Michael Gou, and Daniel Park. 2013. "Stock Market Crash of 1929." Federal Reserve History. https://www.federalreservehistory.org/essays/stock-market-crash-of-1929.

8. Richardson, Gary. 2013. "The Great Depression." Federal Reserve History. https://www.federalreservehistory.org/essays/great-depression.

9. Richardson, Gary. 2013. "The Great Depression." Federal Reserve History. https://www.federalreservehistory.org/essays/great-depression.

10. U.S. Department of Justice. 2020. "Wells Fargo Agrees to Pay $3 Billion to Resolve Criminal and Civil Investigations into Sales Practices Involving the Opening of Millions of Accounts without Customer Authorization." Department of Justice. https://www.justice.gov/opa/pr/wells-fargo-agrees-pay-3-billion-resolve-criminal-and-civil-investigations-sales-practices.

11. Taleb, Nassim N. 2008. *The Black Swan: The Impact of the Highly Improbable.* N.p.: Random House Publishing Group.

12. United States Environmental Protection Agency. 2024. "Deepwater Horizon – BP Gulf of Mexico Oil Spill." United States Environmental Protection Agency. https://www.epa.gov/enforcement/deepwater-horizon-bp-gulf-mexico-oil-spill.

13. United States Environmental Protection Agency. 2024. "Deepwater Horizon – BP Gulf of Mexico Oil Spill." United States Environmental Protection Agency. https://www.epa.gov/enforcement/deepwater-horizon-bp-gulf-mexico-oil-spill.

14. Kaplan, Robert S., Herman B. Leonard, and Anette Mikes. 2020. "The Risks You Can't Forsee." *Harvard Business Review* (November-December). https://hbr.org/2020/11/the-risks-you-cant-foresee.

CHAPTER 8

1. IBM. n.d. "What is Artificial Intelligence (AI)?" IBM. Accessed August 4, 2024. https://www.ibm.com/topics/artificial-intelligence.

2. Ofgang, Eric. 2024. "Piecing together an ancient epic was slow work. Until A.I. got involved." *The New York Times*, August 12, 2024. https://www.nytimes.com/2024/08/12/books/booksupdate/ai-ancient-tablets-gilgamesh.html?

3. Ofgang, Eric. 2024. "Piecing together an ancient epic was slow work. Until A.I. got involved." *The New York Times*, August 12, 2024. https://www.nytimes.com/2024/08/12/books/booksupdate/ai-ancient-tablets-gilgamesh.html?

4. Ofgang, Eric. 2024. "Piecing together an ancient epic was slow work. Until A.I. got involved." *The New York Times*, August 12, 2024. https://www.nytimes.com/2024/08/12/books/booksupdate/ai-ancient-tablets-gilgamesh.html?

5. MIT Sloan Teaching & Learning Technologies. n.d. "When AI Gets It Wrong: Addressing AI Hallucinations and Bias." MIT Sloan Teaching & Learning Technologies. Accessed August 13, 2024. https://mitsloanedtech.mit.edu/ai/basics/addressing-ai-hallucinations-and-bias/.

6. MIT Sloan Teaching & Learning Technologies. n.d. "When AI Gets It Wrong: Addressing AI Hallucinations and Bias." MIT Sloan Teaching & Learning Technologies. Accessed August 13, 2024. https://mitsloanedtech.mit.edu/ai/basics/addressing-ai-hallucinations-and-bias/.

CHAPTER 9

1. Chermack, Thomas J., Susan A. Lynham, and Wendy E. Ruona. 2001. "A Review of Scenario Planning Literature." *Futures Research Quarterly* 17, no. 2 (Summer): 7-32.

2. Chermack, Thomas J., Susan A. Lynham, and Wendy E. Ruona. 2001. "A Review of Scenario Planning Literature." *Futures Research Quarterly* 17, no. 2 (Summer): 7-32.

3. Chermack, Thomas J., Susan A. Lynham, and Wendy E. Ruona. 2001. "A Review of Scenario Planning Literature." *Futures Research Quarterly* 17, no. 2 (Summer): 7-32.

4. Chermack, Thomas J., Susan A. Lynham, and Wendy E. Ruona. 2001. "A Review of Scenario Planning Literature." *Futures Research Quarterly* 17, no. 2 (Summer): 7-32.

5. Akers, Torey. 2024. "University of New Hampshire permanently closes its art museum amid budget cuts." *The Art Newspaper*, January 25, 2024. https://www.theartnewspaper.com/2024/01/25/university-new-hampshire-closes-art-museum-permanently.

6. Akers, Torey. 2024. "University of New Hampshire permanently closes its art museum amid budget cuts." *The Art Newspaper*, January 25, 2024. https://www.theartnewspaper.com/2024/01/25/university-new-hampshire-closes-art-museum-permanently.

7. Smithsonian. 2021. "Smithsonian To Receive Historic $200 Million Donation From Jeff Bezos." National Air and Space Museum. https://airandspace.si.edu/newsroom/press-releases/smithsonian-receive-historic-200-million-donation-jeff-bezos.

8. Smithsonian. 2021. "Smithsonian To Receive Historic $200 Million Donation From Jeff Bezos." National Air and Space Museum. https://airandspace.si.edu/newsroom/press-releases/smithsonian-receive-historic-200-million-donation-jeff-bezos.

9. Smithsonian. 2021. "Smithsonian To Receive Historic $200 Million Donation From Jeff Bezos." National Air and Space Museum. https://airandspace.si.edu/newsroom/press-releases/smithsonian-receive-historic-200-million-donation-jeff-bezos.

10. Goddard, Taegan. 2024. "Washington Monument Strategy." Political Dictionary. https://politicaldictionary.com/words/washington-monument-strategy/.

11. Goddard, Taegan. 2024. "Washington Monument Strategy." Political Dictionary. https://politicaldictionary.com/words/washington-monument-strategy/.

CHAPTER 10

1. PM Magazine. 2014. "Multiyear Budgeting." ICMA. https://icma.org/articles/pm-magazine/multiyear-budgeting.

2. PM Magazine. 2014. "Multiyear Budgeting." ICMA. https://icma.org/articles/pm-magazine/multiyear-budgeting.

3. PM Magazine. 2014. "Multiyear Budgeting." ICMA. https://icma.org/articles/pm-magazine/multiyear-budgeting.

4. PM Magazine. 2014. "Multiyear Budgeting." ICMA. https://icma.org/articles/pm-magazine/multiyear-budgeting.

5. PM Magazine. 2014. "Multiyear Budgeting." ICMA. https://icma.org/articles/pm-magazine/multiyear-budgeting.

Index

Note: Page locators in italics refer to figures and tables.

About the Authors

Ashley Amos is a museum finance leader based in Washington, D.C. She has a BS in business administration, a BA in international studies from the University of Missouri, and a JD from the University of California-Los Angeles.

Jon Carver is a Maryland-based museum chief financial officer. He holds a BA in history and a masters degree in management from the George Washington University.

www.ingramcontent.com/pod-product-compliance
Ingram Content Group UK Ltd.
Pitfield, Milton Keynes, MK11 3LW, UK
UKHW050944290926
15470UKWH00005B/1635

9 781538 198308